When Your Centerpiece is Made of Play-Doh and The Dog Has Eaten Your Crayons

A Mother's Perspective on Parenting

Jennifer M. Koontz

ISBN-10: 1467906131
ISBN-13: 9781467906135

Library of Congress Control Number: 2011960305
CreateSpace, North Charleston, SC

For Nancy Koontz,
who taught by example and
loved unconditionally

Table of Contents

Chapter One:
Allow Me to Introduce Myself

I've been a parent for almost six years. I am no expert, but as a mom and a teacher, I can't help but make observations about life, parenthood, and how to combine the two. This is a parenting book, but not in the typical sense of the word. It may teach you about parenting, but not about subjects like vaccinations and potty training. I wrote this book for all parents, no matter their age, stage, or background, to remind them how important it is to keep things in perspective and find the humor in the many lessons that they will learn along the way. Not only can we raise kind and respectful children, but we can be kind and respectful too. All at the same time.

Parenting is an adventure as well as a great source of material for storytelling. We parents need a parenting book that is not so much a "How to" book as it is a "Wow, I need to remember that" book. And beyond that, we need some humor in our lives. Parenting can be fun, and funny, if we allow it to be. I also wrote this book as a reminder to all of us that children are wonderful teachers and that we have so much to learn from them.

I will admit to you right up front that I am a rather uptight mother. I am married to a man who is a rather uptight father. We are *up tight*. We were that way before we were parents, and we are that way now. Uptight parents are well-meaning and conscientious, but they need to remember to laugh. They need to read books on parenting and ask questions of a wide variety of people who are also parents. They need their children to teach them how to parent, and most of all, they need to know that the world will not come to an end (and their children will continue to grow), even if things don't go according to plan every day.

Let me tell you the story of how I learned one of my very first lessons about being a parent. My husband and I adopted our daughter. She came to us at nine and a half months old after having been cared for by a wonderful foster family. My husband brought her home to me, as I am not a good traveler and an even worse flyer. I will forever be grateful to him for offering to travel far away to meet people who would judge what kind of father he would be as he met and attempted to bond with an infant who didn't know him from Adam. He made this trip virtually alone, and he managed it like a pro. This husband of mine, he is my hero.

I met my daughter for the first time in the baggage claim area of BWI Airport in Baltimore. I walked in the door to the baggage claim area, looked straight ahead, and there they were. My husband always carried our daughter high on his shoulder, and as such, I could see her perfectly. I thought *There's my daughter. Hmmm. Funny hair. Wow, she's so small. Will those six-to-nine-month clothes that I bought really fit her? Why is her hair sticking up like a chimpanzee?*

What a strange collection of thoughts, right? I had planned for nine and a half months what I would think when I first saw my daughter, and instead, *that* string of thoughts is what ran through my mind. (Note to reader: Yes, I actually planned what I would THINK when I met my daughter.)

Nevertheless, the most wonderful moment of my life was when my husband handed our daughter to me and simultaneously exclaimed, "I've got to find a restroom!" As he sought out the facilities, I stood in the middle of the baggage claim area saying over and over, "I'm your mommy. I'm your mommy. I'm your mommy." Part of me wanted to say those words to her so that she would know it was true, and part of me couldn't believe the sound of it! Tears were streaming down my face, relief and fear and gratitude were all mixing together to create a beautiful moment of extreme joy. She was mine, she was home, and...and...and...then I felt it.

I was wet from my neck to my thighs. At that time, my husband was not adept at the whole diapering thing, and though he had returned from his trip to the men's room, I was not about to ask him when he changed our daughter's diaper last. The poor guy was exhausted and not prepared for a diaper interrogation. So because the ladies room was miles away, I looked around quickly and discovered an empty hallway nearby.

I prepared the spot with many layers of diaper pads and proceeded to change our daughter on the floor of the airport. On the floor—in the baggage claim of BWI airport. She screamed the whole time, people stared, and the six-to-nine-month outfit that I brought along did not fit after all. The legs of the outfit hung down about six inches lower than the bottom of her feet.

The first diaper change experience was successful in that it got the job done, but it was not ideal in any sense of the word. What did I learn? That parenting is all about winging it. It's all about making do and making the best of things. It's about going into each situation well prepared with a great plan, but always being ready to make a quick change. Literally.

Chapter Two:

Babies, Bottles, and the Truth

Babies. Puh. What do I know about babies? Our lovely little one came to us after the newborn stage, even nearing the end of the infant stage. So in many ways, I remain very much a novice where babies are concerned. The thing is I have had the honor of watching and learning from some of the best parents around. And because our daughter really was still a baby when she came to us, she did have time to teach me a few things.

Babies are a mystery to me, and I suspect I'm not alone. They inspire both love and resentment, sometimes in the very same day, or at least on consecutive days. The little one who melted your heart when he smiled at you on Monday can really get on your nerves on Tuesday. Why? Because he did not let you get any sleep on Monday night.

Sometimes babies do things that make us think that they understand kindness. They laugh that adorable, engaging belly laugh just at the time when we need to hear laughter. They seem interested in baseball because they know we love the sport. They sit and look at a catalog with us when we really need some new navy blue pumps. Then, a very short time later, there is just no reasoning with them. They want what they want. No apologies, no excuses. It's just their nature. Sometimes they give, sometimes they take. Here is the important thing to remember: when babies are babies, the day-to-day routine takes over your life and your mind. It isn't until they are not babies anymore that you realize how much giving they actually did. It's important to keep it all in perspective and appreciate what you have when you have it.

When I was a child, I always heard the grown-ups talk about how fast the time goes. Now, every time I turn around, someone is telling me to enjoy my child now, because the time goes by so fast. To the people who are inclined to say such things to new parents, this is for you: WE KNOW THAT. We know it, and we hate it. It inspires every emotion from wistfulness to despair. Parents, especially mothers, do not tend to live in the moment. We are so busy planning the next moment that we tend to deny ourselves the privilege of living in the present moment.

When my daughter had been home with us for a week or so, I held her in the evenings and she fell asleep on me. For many of you, that may not seem like a monumental occurrence. You may have multiple children and have had babies sleeping on you for years. You may still think it's cute, but it has ceased to be elevated in your mind to miracle status. To me, it was a miracle. She was mine. She was here. She was sleeping.

That stage slipped away so quickly. Within a short time, she was crawling, and everyone knows what that means. She spent all day and night dry mopping my hardwood floors with the knees of her pants, and when she was tired, it was time for her to be really asleep, in her crib, not lounging around on Mom or Dad. I was so proud of my little one, crawling around so fast and discovering the world at lightning speed.

Still, my focus always seemed to be on what would come next. What I didn't stop to realize was that I was missing the present. I had almost missed the snuggling stage. I had participated in it, yes, but I was not fully *there*. I wasn't living in that moment because I was spending so much time thinking about whether the next moment would be okay. If only I could go back in time and simply tell myself, "Enjoy this. Everything will be okay." So now, as often as I can, I try to remind myself (and any new parents I meet) to enjoy the adventures as they occur.

The thing about babies is that they grow. If only I had spent more time noticing the tiny things, like how she twirled the hair near her ear when she was getting sleepy and how she laughed when our little pug ran in wild circles around the dining room table. I want to see those things again, but I can't. They're gone, everywhere but in my memory.

The stages slip away so quickly, and we need to pay attention. There are so many things that we would like to say to our children when they are too young to really understand. Baby books and scrapbooks are great; I am all in favor of them. They mark the milestones and the gifts that were given over the years. But they don't really record our thoughts, our feelings, and our wisdom. And by the time our children are old enough to understand that wisdom, there is a good chance we will have forgotten it!

So here is a suggestion that has become so important to me. Take a few minutes, maybe once a month and on particularly special days throughout the year, to write a letter to your little one. Nothing fancy, just pretend that your child is grown and you are talking to her as if she were grown. Tell her what you know. Tell her what she does now, how you look forward to seeing how it will progress, and what you have learned. I even wrote my daughter a letter one day when I was angry with her. Why not? Fifteen or twenty years from now, she'll probably find it amusing to know what made her mom angry when she was a toddler. I always write her a letter on her birthday and on New Year's Eve, just as the clock strikes midnight.

I wrote these letters for her, to her, but I have enjoyed them immensely. They teach me, every time I read them, that I had so much to learn, but I already knew so much. Sometimes I think about when I will give the letters to her. Will it be when she is a teenager, and she screams at me that I don't really care about her? Will it be when she leaves our home to go away to school or the night before her wedding? Or maybe I'll wait until she has a child of her own? I figure I'll know when the time is right. I'll also know that this is one thing that I did right as a parent. There will be many things I'll wish I could do over, but writing her letters is one thing that I know I won't regret.

Bottles

Whereas it is so important to keep the experiences of "babyhood" in perspective, as I have described above, it is also important to stay calm when faced with the myriad of products that are available to, um, make your life easier.

Do you know what intimidated me the most when I was a new mother? Baby bottles. There are so many of them! Have you perused the baby department in a superstore and taken a good look at the many brands and models and apparatuses having to do with the administration of baby nourishment? If you were not feeling overwhelmed before you looked at the baby bottle section, you very well could be after you try to figure out which one you should actually buy for your baby.

You think to yourself, *This is really important. I've got to get this right. I want my baby to feel comfortable and loved, and eating is pretty important to a baby.* The next thoughts might be, *Oh geez, I don't know what I'm doing. Everyone else standing here looking at this stuff seems to know exactly what they need. I am a well-educated adult and I haven't a clue. There are slow flow nipples, fast flow nipples, bottles that are slanted, and some that are supposedly shaped like a woman's breast. How am I supposed to pick one of these bottles? Maybe I should get one of each. No, no, I can't do that! That will confuse the baby. I can't do this. What made me think I could raise a child?"* All of this angst over a container that holds liquid!

And it's not just baby bottles that are overwhelming. It's all of the products and all of the choices. If you're approaching panic attack mode in the baby bottle aisle, just wait until you proceed to the aisle with the baby formula and diapers. Whoa, Nelly! What do all of those letters mean on the front of the formula cans? Are we supposed to know instinctively which type of formula will be the best one? Then, as if infant formula isn't confusing enough, now there are products that seem to be formulated for older babies. How do we know if we need that? How about baby vitamins?

Okay, okay, you say to yourself, *I'll worry about the formula later. Let me look at the diaper aisle for a few minutes. How hard can that be?* Round the corner with your cart and you'll see that the diaper aisle is even worse than the formula aisle! They are all expensive, but some are reasonably expensive, and some are out-of-this-world outrageously expensive. *Do I need to buy the most expensive one to get a good quality? Is elastic really necessary?*

And then, as your eyes wander to the diapering products, you think this: *What in the name of all that's holy is "Butt Paste"?* Ewwwww. Don't worry, you don't have to use Butt Paste if you don't care for the sound of it, but the products you will find yourself using over the years are likely to help you overcome any squeamishness relating to bodies or bodily fluids. It's just amazing what can come out of those adorable, cooing little bundles of joy.

Let the baby product anxiety be a metaphor for every situation you will face in raising your child. Our culture is filled with choices, which almost everyone agrees is a good thing. Choices are good. Confusion is not good. It makes you feel like a ninny when you can't choose a type of bottle, a brand of formula, or a diaper style for your own child. How will you feel when it's time to choose a pediatrician or a preschool?

How do we keep the adventures of babyhood in perspective and manage the choices that are presented to us? We *ask for help.* We find people whom we respect and whom we feel know a fair amount about parenting, and we ask them what products they selected and what advice they can offer. In times past, young mothers depended on their own mothers and sisters to inaugurate them into the motherhood club. Now we need to look outside of our immediate families for advice. Many of us have mothers, sisters, aunts, and cousins who are wise, but the products and trends have changed and evolved.

As for the many product choices available to us, I propose that we follow a few basic rules:

1. Find someone you respect, someone who has navigated these waters recently, and ask, ask, ask. This person has been through it all—and recently. Then, if you feel it's necessary, get a second opinion.

2. Keep your receipts. If you are unhappy with a product and you explain the problem while you present the receipt, stores will usually let you exchange a product that isn't working for you.

3. Everything in life is about trial and error. Whether we're talking baby bottles or choices that are much more significant, all we can do is gather information, ask a few people for their opinions, and then go with the one that seems the most reasonable.

If your child is consistently unhappy with your choice, whether it's a bottle or something more significant, listen to your child. That is not being indulgent; it is being responsible. Our children teach us a lot about parenting if we pay attention.

The Truth

I love it when authors title part of their book "The Truth." It makes me feel as though I am about to be given an amazing piece of information. A true pearl. And in this case, I *am* going to give you a true pearl of wisdom.

The truth is this: the way to survive parenthood is to do what works for you. Simple, yes, but so very true. Keeping parenthood in perspective relates to everything from appreciating every day and every stage to controlling the panic when faced with the barrage of products that beckon to you as a new parent. Whether you are in the baby stage, the toddler stage, or beyond, parents must do whatever it takes to make it through the day and night. That is *The Truth.*

The caveat to this pearl of wisdom is that we must do whatever it takes, within reason. I'm a firm believer in tough love, and "doing whatever it takes" does not mean allowing a child to get away with anything as long as she'll quiet down. That is not at all what I mean. The amazing truth that I have just revealed only works if you use it alongside common sense.

Here is a small example of doing whatever it takes to get through the day: I am dedicated to the idea that children should be fed nutritious foods, complete with protein, fruits, and vegetables. I mention these three in particular because they are the ones that are often the hardest to get children to eat. I am not a fanatic, mind you. I could do a lot better searching out whole grains and organic foods. (I am going to work on that, by the way.)

I have spent most of my life battling a weight problem, and I would like to do everything I can to help my daughter make good choices. We talk about choosing foods that are good for her body and which foods are okay to eat only on special occasions. (The special occasion thing is dicey, however, because this child of mine can create a holiday out of nothing. She believes that finding a puddle to step into constitutes a reason for celebration. In her mind, the Puddle Celebration Day should be celebrated with corn dogs.)

At first, when she ate her food from jars (those were the days!), it was easy to balance her meals. She ate everything, including vegetables. She loved everything I fed her. It was wonderful, and we were both happy. Then, as time passed, her exuberance for vegetables waned, and I was left with the very common plight of the mother whose child doesn't want to eat her veggies.

So in order to "do what works," I did this: early on, I did not refer to baby food jars as "baby food." I fed her applesauce from my jar of adult applesauce and called it "sauce." Then I began calling everything of that texture "sauce," including the baby food veggies, cereals, and fruits. So if I feel that she has not had enough veggies in a certain day, I tell her that she must pick a "sauce" to eat before anything else will be served. She gets to pick, and I get her to eat nutritious foods to balance out the rest of her diet.

I did not publicize to many people the fact that my four-year-old daughter still ate baby food on occasion, and I realized that those halcyon days would not last forever. It helped me, though, for a while. And that's all that mattered at the time.

The truth is that sometimes we make parenting far more complicated than it needs to be. Let's keep the many choices and opinions in perspective. Opinions, including those contained in this book, are just that. Choices and opinions don't have to launch us into a frenzy if we trust our intuition to lead us in the right direction.

Once you find what works to get you through the day (and night), keep an open mind to new ideas, but trust in your own wisdom to know what is best for your family. And that's *The Truth.* Do whatever works to help you make it through the day and keep it in perspective. Find the humor in it. And by all means, remind yourself to enjoy this. Everything will be okay.

Chapter Three:

Who Is This Little Person?

What kind of question is that? Who is this person? This person is my child. Nobody knows this person better than I do. I am this person's parent, how can you ask such a thing?

I ask such a thing because it is natural to get a little defensive when someone asks you about your child and you realize that, deep down, if all truth were revealed, you really don't know. It's time to change that.

To figure out what and who your little person is, it is necessary to observe the little tyke in motion and at rest. You need to become one of those people who wears a khaki-colored safari jacket, sport some binoculars, and, most importantly, record valuable data in a field journal. You're on a mission.

The first thing you must do to really learn your kid is to clear your mind. I know, easier said than done. But your mission is to learn who your child really is, not *who you would like your child to be*. Be honest, you know that you have some preconceived ideas of who you would like your child to be, even if you vowed that you would never be that sort of parent.

I used to say that my daughter's academic achievement was not important to me. I wanted her to learn to be a compassionate, content person, happy with her choices and proud of herself. Sounds good, no? It's true. I really do want those things. But in the deep recesses of my mind, I really wanted her to be a ballroom dancing, ice skating musician and singer who happened to enjoy her career as a heart surgeon in one of the top teaching hospitals in the country.

How do we avoid having expectations for children whom we love so much? We want the world for them. For me, it's not so much that I care about my child's achievement; it's more that I want her to feel the pride of achievement and accept the accolades of people who appreciate her effort. I want her to know what it feels like to be proud of herself. I want that because I've had it, and it's a powerful, wonderful feeling.

Still, to be the kind of parent I want to be, the kind we all should be, I need to let go of my notions of what "successful" should mean for her. "Why?" you say. Because if we are holding desires and expectations for our children, they will know it. They will sense it, and it will become a burden to them. Instead of achieving what is important to them, they will always, at least in part, be trying to please us. To love unconditionally, which is what I aim for every day, is to love a child for his or her choices, not for accomplishing the choices that we have made on their behalf.

I just wrote a long section about why I want my child to achieve great things, and then I was reminded of something my husband said to my daughter when she was a baby. (This demonstrates the difference between my husband and me.) He held her up, looked into her eyes, and said, "When you grow up, you don't have to be successful if you don't want to. It's okay. You can live here with Mommy and Daddy forever if you want to."

What a daddy, right? Who wouldn't want to hear something like that from their father? My husband is the type of man who usually lives in the present. He doesn't worry about setting a fifteen-year plan or what we will say when it's time to talk to our daughter about sex, drugs, and rock 'n roll. Sometimes this is not such a great thing, because he's not always the best at navigating the "what ifs." Then again, why should he be? He's got me for that. But for a parent to be able to say to a child, "Find your happiness. We'll be right behind you. We've got your back," which is in essence what he was saying to her, is huge. For children to become their own little people, they need us to let them find their happiness, know that we support them, and trust that we'll be there for them if they need us.

Raise your hand if you've mastered that. Okay, nobody believes you, so put your hand down. All we can do is try to be the parents that we want to be. Sure, we let our children know that we expect them to be respectful, gentle, conscientious, and responsible, but beyond that, we step aside and let them find what makes them happy. If it sounds to you like I have that lesson well under control, well, keep reading.

Play-Doh and Crayons

Picture this...I'm sitting at the kitchen table, craft supplies set out on the table in little dishes and bowls. The glitter pens are all lined up, the construction paper and crayons stand at the ready. My daughter and I are going to do CRAFTS. I have looked forward to this for years. I was never particularly good at art, but I loved crafts. Craft supplies, really. Oh, the supplies. When I was young, we had crayons and paper. Markers, if we were lucky. (I'm not even really that old, but boy, has the art supply industry exploded with great ideas over the last twenty years.) I'm sitting at the kitchen table, having covered it nicely with a plastic tablecloth before setting out my beloved supplies, and I wait.

I am waiting for my daughter to come, because all morning I had been telling her that if she was a good girl and cooperated, we would have time to do crafts. She didn't look overly excited at the prospect, but she didn't decline the invitation either. So I took that to mean, "Sure, Mom, let's make some stuff." I was psyched.

So here I wait.

Where is she, anyway? I finally go look for her. She's not in her bedroom. Not in her playroom. Not in any of the usual spots. Then I hear music from downstairs. Rock music, specifically the song "American Woman." I hear guitar and maybe even drums. Now I get it. Now I understand. Playing "air guitar" with Dad has trumped doing crafts with Mom. How dare she! Doesn't she realize that I am waiting—and have been waiting since she was, oh, just about one year old? (Come to think of it, aren't I always waiting?) She doesn't want to do what I think will be fun. She wants to do what she thinks will be fun. And that's playing in a *faux* rock band with her dad.

Feeling rejected, jealous, and all of the other emotions that demonstrate how *not* grown up I really am, I go back to my craft table. I clean up the supplies, keep my chin up, and hope that one day my girl will say, "C'mon, Mom, let's make some stuff." They say hope is what keeps us going, so I decide that, by golly, I will just wait for that day.

I begin putting the little sequins back into their baggies and the silk rosettes back in their proper place when I happen to notice that the line of crayons is noticeably shorter than it was before I left for the "rock concert." When I look to the other side of the kitchen, I see our pug, Meg, chewing. She isn't just chewing, either, she is chomping. Crayons entitled "Laser Lemon," "Neon Carrot," "Sky Blue, "Electric Lime," and a lovely shade of brown called "Burnt Sienna"— she chomps them all. I quickly yell, "No!" then grab the few uneaten nubs of crayon, throw them in the trash, and wash my hands. The crayons are slimy from her saliva. As I wash my hands, I can feel tears coming, but I know I'm being oversensitive, so I remind myself that plenty of people have told me that my daughter will want to spend time with me one day. They promised. Really.

I put the dog in the laundry room and close the door, partly because I want the whole fiasco to be out of sight and out of mind and partly because I don't know how digestible crayons actually are. I know they're advertised as being "non-toxic," but I have never heard anyone claim that they're "digestible."

I'm sure you can tell where this little crayon scenario is headed, if you've ever had a dog—and especially if you've had a dog that ate your crayons. Later that day, our pug went outside to do what dogs do outside (if you're lucky), and my daughter was watching her out the window. I was busily chopping celery for that evening's dinner when my daughter turned to me and said, "Mom, is that a rainbow?"

I said, "No, honey, rainbows come after rain showers."

She said, "No, Meg just made one!"

I rushed over to the window and saw that she was right. Meg had not made a rainbow. She had made a yard full of rainbows.

For those of you who may be wondering, Meg was just fine after the storm passed, so to speak, and my daughter went back to whatever it was she was doing, not at all concerned by the "rainbows" or by the fact that her mommy was feeling rejected. She was perfectly satisfied with the choices she had made that day.

I learned something valuable that day. Actually, I learn something valuable most every day, but on that particular day, I learned that I can hope that my daughter shares my interests, I can pray that she will want to spend time with me sometime in her life, but I cannot make her into something she is not. I cannot make her want to do crafts with me if becoming a "rocker" is her passion. For a control freak like me, that's a tough one, but I'm working on it. And if I forget for a little while, she'll help me to remember. Kids are great that way.

And As They Grow…

Wouldn't it be great if we could just say to our children, "How do you do? Lovely to meet you. Welcome to our home. Tell us a little bit about yourself."? I think that would be great. It would save us so much time, not to mention the expense of the safari jacket, binoculars, and field journal that I mentioned at the beginning of this chapter.

And it would be even better if we could ask those questions on a regular basis as our children grow, just so we can keep ourselves apprised of, let's say, "current events." The reality is, however, that we cannot just ask our children who they are and what they like, because often times they don't know. Or even if they know, they don't know how to explain it to us. It's our job to do the work of learning to know our children, and it's impossible to parent well if you don't know your child. And by *know* your child, I mean *understand* your child.

There are countless books out there that teach parents how to know their children, how to understand their children, and how to manage their children. They are good books, written by experts who are infinitely well-versed in the art of child interpretation. The difference between those books and this one is that many of those books teach parents how to interpret phases of child development and relate them to what they see at home. Me? I'm just trying to get through the day. I just want to figure out what will work for us today so that we can make it peacefully to tomorrow (when, maybe, *someone* will want to do crafts with me).

In all seriousness, though, we need to know our children so we can learn how to work with them, not for them or against them. Parents and children can work as a team. There can be cooperation in a household if parents and children understand each other. We need to "learn" our children, for sure, but read on to discover why I am not a fan of "learning by labeling."

The Time for Labeling Has Expired

My friend has what is called a "strong-willed child." When she learned that, she bought every book out there to help her understand the affliction with which her son had just been diagnosed. She read with a highlighter in hand, and she also began seeing a child psychologist to help her learn to parent a child of the strong-willed variety. She signed up to learn about play therapy. And she became terribly depressed. The more depressed she became, the less able she was to interact with her strong-willed son.

I would like to caution parents about our culture's obsession with labeling children. Every child seems to be labeled gifted, reluctant, introverted, extroverted, or (heaven forbid) perverted. "Strong willed" is yet another label that strikes fear in the hearts of parents because it suggests to them that their child is a problem now, or is sure to be a problem in the future. Please know that I am not opposed to labeling for the purpose of diagnosing a child if the child has a condition that requires medical attention. Some labels are necessary—if treatment follows. Aside from that, beware of becoming swept up in the "label maker" that is our society.

A mother I know told me a story that illustrates the problem with labeling children. When her son was around six, he was in the basement recreation room with his dad and a group of his dad's friends, watching them play pool. At one point, her son was standing too close to the pool table and an errant pool ball hit him in the forehead. He blacked out, was taken to the hospital, and developed quite a bump on his head. When he awoke in the emergency room, the nurse talked to him about the incident. She said to him, "That's quite a bump you've got on your head. I'll bet when that pool ball hit you, you really saw stars." The little boy replied, "No, no stars. Just the ceiling. I was in the basement!"

The little boy in this story could have been described as "literal" by those who love to create labels. *Literal* means that things are interpreted to represent exactly what they are called. The little boy in the story thought that the nurse really believed he had seen stars. He didn't recognize that the phrase "saw stars" really meant "experienced a major jolt to the head."

As a teacher, I have grown used to the labeling of children. And I hate it. If the little boy in the story had been labeled "literal," it's likely that someone would have had suggestions for his parents about how to deal with a literal child. News flash: ALL children are literal! Until their vocabularies develop enough to include the varying meanings of phrases such as "seeing stars" and they can exist in a world of intangibility, they are literal beings. What good does it do to label a child (and perhaps try to change the child) when most children are that way?

To me, this is an example of our society becoming too anxious to place a child in a category. Why do we do this? I believe it's because we want answers—fast. Therefore, we rush to have our children "tested" so that we can begin to "treat" them. Again, if it involves a medical diagnosis that requires medical treatment, I'm all in favor of it. But sometimes, rather than labeling a child so quickly, we need to stand back and study them a little longer. Notice that I didn't say, "Stand back and do nothing." I said, "Stand back and study them." There is a difference.

As a teacher and now a parent, I notice that our society, our educators, mental health professionals, and parents are so quick to make a "diagnosis." Sometimes therapists reach conclusions about a child's personality type and supposed problems after watching them play with plastic superheroes for forty-five minutes!

I promised you at the beginning of this book that I am a believer in common sense and humor, when appropriate. Labeling children, to me, is humorous (read "ludicrous") because, as in the story above, the labels rarely help us. Often what labels do is cause panic, and we all know that panic never helps. We communicate best with our children when we know who they are and what motivates them. A label does very little to help us "learn" our children. Observation, interaction, communication, invention, and diversion—those are the things that teach us the most about our kids.

Chapter Four:

They Really Are Actual People

Common sense tells me that my child is an individual. Unique, with a variety of strengths, challenges, and quirks. Your goal, and mine, should be to meet our children where they are, *know* them as individuals, and refrain from grouping them into any category or personality type. I feel sure that some people will disagree with me on this point, but that's okay. I told you that these are my opinions. And here are some more...

Your child is your child, and as such, you must learn to know him, understand him, and then move toward the ultimate goal—helping him to become a happy, healthy, functioning part of society. Having a strong-willed child (or an extrovert or an introvert) is no reason to despair. Think of it as an invitation to study a subject that wasn't offered in school. You have a living, breathing alien living in your home and you have been given the honor of helping that alien grow into a productive member of society.

As a teacher, I always found the difficult students to be some of the most interesting ones. By "difficult," I mean surly, uninterested, and behaviorally challenged. Sometimes the best way to figure out a child is to pay attention to what the child does *not* like. Ask yourself (and then record in your field journal) what conditions and circumstances do not work for your child. When does your child have a meltdown? What happens before his behavior goes south? What things do you say to your child that inspires stubbornness, irrational behavior, and just plain crabbiness? Sometimes when we aren't sure what does work, it's easier to begin by looking at what doesn't work.

For example, if you have a child who does not respond to spanking, why do it? (Spanking, by the way, rarely inspires the desired result. Have you ever seen a child stop crying after he received a spanking? I haven't.) If your child is nasty and demanding late in the afternoon, think about whether he could be hungry, tired, or both. If you collect your child from school and he is demanding and cranky, that is not the time to teach him a lesson on good manners.

As they say, timing is everything. Any child, of any "type," is not going to respond positively to conditions that are unfavorable to him. Also, children learn and react differently. Some learn by listening, some by touching, some by reading, and so on. If you try to interact with your child in a way that is uncomfortable or frustrating to him, you are not going to have success. If you yell at your child more often than you would like, think about what response you get from your child. Some children get mad, some get scared, some don't respond at all. If you pay attention to the way your child responds to you and the circumstances surrounding the response, you will begin to notice patterns.

The reason that I suggested you begin by identifying what your child doesn't like is that it produces the fastest results. It is usually fairly clear when a child doesn't like something. If you can identify a method of communicating you are using that your child doesn't respond to, you can make a change in your behavior and your expectations.

I know a mother who does not expect anything of her children for the first thirty minutes after they arrive home from school. Backpacks get tossed on the floor, school clothes and shoes are not put away immediately, and her expectations of that period of time are simply to get the children home, get them changed into play clothes, and feed them a healthy snack. She listens to their news of the day, and then, once they are fed and have had a few minutes to rest, her expectations for a neat house return. The children put their things away much more willingly than they would if she shouted at them to do so as soon as they walked in the door.

When you come to know your child, you can anticipate his or her needs and behaviors. As grown-ups, instead of constantly expecting change from our children, perhaps it is we who must make the changes, at least temporarily. If we work to understand the sources of friction, then we can adjust our expectations. Note that I did not say that we should abandon our expectations. Trust me, I am chock full of expectations. But the key is to better match our expectations to our children's capabilities at any given moment. If we don't take the time to learn our children and plow on with our own agendas, there will not be peace in our homes.

In generations past, parents did not work to accommodate their children. We know now that fostering a "team" spirit within the family creates stronger and more loving bonds later in life. So, to create a team spirit, get to know your teammates and respect them. Make adjustments in your expectations so that everyone gets what they need. Not only will your children appreciate it, they will learn how it's done.

Look Out…You're Being Watched Too

As we learn about our children, they're learning to know us too. Be careful, you're being watched! When you begin to see mannerisms that you use or phrases that you utter coming from the mouth of your little one, it will most likely affect you in some way. Hopefully it will evoke amusement when you see yourself mirrored in your child's actions and speech. Or, quite possibly, you could be mortified to see the least flattering side of you mimicked by your child.

When my nephew was a little guy of approximately two years, he was looking out the open window in the dining room, which faces the front of the home. Some guests were coming up the walk toward the front porch when my nephew shouted to his mother, "Who the hell is that?" I know that my sister would have rather done anything at that moment to avoid opening the front door!

Most of us have had our language parroted at least once, and it can be a real eye-opener. Children don't just parrot profanity; they parrot phrasing, tone of voice, and context. Recently I heard my daughter say, "I might as well..." several times throughout the day. I remember thinking *I wonder where she learned that phrase.* It wasn't until several days later that I heard myself preface many comments with, "I might as well..." I have probably been doing that for years, but I wasn't aware of it until I heard my daughter say it too.

Children are not just learning the way we talk; they are learning to interpret body language. My daughter can tell the exact moment that I begin to get upset. If I'm upset and begin to get teary, she turns her head to look at me quickly and then dashes from the room. The first time she did this, I felt even worse, thinking that my emotional state had really upset her. A moment later she came running back into the room with a tissue and brought it right over to me. Then the tears really began to flow.

Another time I passed through her bedroom after she had gone to school and noticed her stuffed giraffe lying on his side with a tissue next to him. He was neatly covered with a doll blanket. When she came home from school, I asked her why the giraffe had a tissue and a blanket. She said, "He was upset that I was leaving and he couldn't go along. I thought he would feel better if I gave him a tissue and covered him up." I was touched by her empathy. She was learning something valuable from me after all.

Keep in mind that our children look to us first as their examples of proper behavior. At times you may think (as I have) that your child refuses to learn from you and pays you no mind at all. Not true. Our children watch us in good times and bad. They watch how we react to every situation. I know of a mother, very outgoing and friendly, who gave a little wave to people who were walking in her neighborhood. One day her daughter asked her why she did that.

"It's a nice thing to do. It makes people happy when you wave to them." A few days later, she noticed her daughter giving a little wave from her car seat to people, cars, trucks, and construction workers that they passed. Her mother then had to give her the talk about when it's okay to talk to people and how to determine who is a stranger, but nevertheless, it showed the mother that children do what we do.

It is for that reason that I must caution parents and other supporters of young sports players. Most of us have heard the stories of parents fighting in the bleachers during a ball game in which their children are involved. To those parents, I say, "How could you involve your child in a sport for the purpose of having them learn about teamwork and good sportsmanship and then proceed to talk trash to other spectators in the stands?" What are the kids learning from the adults who insult each other and argue with the referees? Adults who think that the kids involved don't notice their behavior are sadly mistaken. Not only do they notice it, they emulate it.

My hope is that we as parents can do a better job of hiding our immaturity in the future. Most of us have not matured much past adolescence, but where raising children is concerned, we must hide that and pretend we are mature grown-ups. We have a responsibility to teach our children right from wrong. The warning that some people give their children—"Do as I say, not as I do"—is not going to cut it. Children do as we do, whether we like it or not. So please, for the sake of all of our children, please "do" good.

How Do We Play?

Now that you have observed your child, taken notes, perhaps altered your approach, *learned* your child, and accepted that he is constantly *learning* you too, it is time for you to go. Go have some fun. Play, be free, enjoy.

"Um...how do I do that?" Yes, that's right—some people honestly don't know how to play. I must admit (I am writing with my head bowed), I am one of those people for whom "playing" does not come naturally. I'm not really sure why that is, other than I have a hard time playing before all the work is done, and for a mom, the work is never done. I have heard so many mothers say that they don't play because they don't have time. It's a shame that mothers rarely allow themselves to be playmates. We don't tend to evaluate the quality of our mothering by the quality of our playtime with our children, but that needs to change.

We absolutely must play with our children, because it teaches them things they will need to know for the future. By playing with our children, we show them that we are not just the ogres who dole out punishments and set bedtimes. We are real people who giggle, fall down, and play kickball, just like them. When they see that we are like them, we earn their trust. Once we earn their trust, they view us as friends, and as they grow, they will be more likely to confide in us about the big stuff. We need to achieve a healthy balance between "authority figure" and "confidante," so that we are in the position to guide them through the teenage years. If we are only authority figures and not confidantes, they are not going to trust us to help them when the big problems come along.

So what do you do if you want to play, you know that you need to play, but it just doesn't go well when you try to do it? You could sign up for a class that teaches "Play Therapy," which I don't fully understand because, well, I never took the class. Or you could try what I am trying.

This is an area where I really need to improve, so I'm approaching it as I do many other areas about which I know next to nothing: I observe people who do it better than I do. One person who is very good at playing lives right here in my household. It's my husband. He has that part of parenting well under control. I watch him play dolls, board games, "air guitar" rock band (of course, you know about that one already), doll house, and just about anything else my daughter wants to play. One time I thought to myself, *I wish I actually enjoyed playing all of those things the way he does.* Then I came to find out a few weeks later that he doesn't. He doesn't like playing all of those things.

Although this is a secret from our daughter, it was a huge revelation to me. I was disappointed because I wasn't having fun playing when all sources told me that I was supposed to have fun. Here is the piece of wisdom that I have gleaned from that: when your goal is to have fun with your children, it does not necessarily mean that you must enjoy playing with their toys. Your joy is derived from their enjoyment. Watch the face, the laughter, the wonder, the satisfaction on your child's face when she is playing something that she enjoys, when she has mastered a minor (or major) skill, and best of all, she has YOU sitting there with her, watching the whole scene. It's the time spent together that creates the fun, not necessarily the actual activity.

So I am learning to treasure playtime as an exercise in "living vicariously." I don't have to love playing everything we play. Whereas we used to argue about what we would play, now we work toward sharing the decision making, and I am working on having fun watching her having fun.

Now my husband, the King of Playtime, would say that you don't have to completely give up having fun with the actual toys—there are ways to make sure that you get to be a kid again, i.e. pick the toys you want to play with, but his philosophy of playing is that kids must learn to enjoy playing with you first. Then you can progress to sharing the decision making over the actual activity that you both will play. Just like everything else in life, first things first.

One of the reasons why I suggest that we observe our children and get to know them is so that we can enjoy them! "Learning" your child is indeed a process that needs to be ongoing. You can never say that you're done learning your child, any more than they are ever done trying to figure you out. But one of your ultimate goals should be to enjoy your time with your child. The way I see it, our job as parents is to make sure our children turn into good people. No easy task. However, if we enjoy spending time with them, then it is probably safe to say that other people will enjoy spending time with them too. I'd say that we're well on our way to the "good person" goal if other people actually want to spend time with our children.

That way, if someone were to ask you, as I did, "Who is this person?" you would be proud to answer, "This is my child. I know him, I like him, and I'd be proud for you to know him too."

Chapter Five:

What Children Wish We Knew

When we become parents, we think we know what to do. We think we've had enough life experience to guide us on our way, and we also think that there are billions of people in the world who somehow grew up, so, really, it can't be all that hard. Still, as our children grow, and we grow too, there are things that our children wish we knew.

When our daughter first came home to us, there were times that she just cried and there didn't seem to be anything that she needed. She was dry, she was fed, she didn't have a fever. We tried all of the things that people suggested we try, but still she cried. As adoptive parents, we were gently warned that adoptive children occasionally grieve the loss of their first care-takers. Children who are adopted make huge adjustments in a short time, and sometimes they simply feel sad. Perhaps we could even describe it as homesickness. Although we as parents wanted to feel as though there was no reason for our child to feel homesick because she was (finally) home with us, her feelings had little to do with us and more to do with the wonderful family she missed.

Nevertheless, we never did figure out why she cried sometimes. We only knew that it was heart-breaking because we wanted to make her feel better and we didn't know how. I believe all parents feel that way sometimes. We try to read our children's minds, but we can't always do it, and it hurts us to think that we can't fix whatever is wrong.

Hence the purpose for this particular chapter: What would they say to us if they had the words? What do children want their parents to know?

The Wee Ones Want Us to Know…

"Hey, Mom and Dad, I'm tired of lying in this one position and looking at the same thing for so long. And stop shaking that thing in my face. It's annoying. A little change of scenery would be great right about now.

"As long as I have your attention, I guess I'd like you to know that I don't mind playing along with the getting-dressed-up-for-the-well-wishers gig, but the incessant ogling can get tiresome too. I would really dig some action. How about one of these oglers taking me for some fresh air?

"Did you know that the two best ways to calm me when I'm out of sorts are to (1) take me outside for a couple of laps around the house, and (2) let me play in some water? Supervised, of course. I don't mean that you should let me play in water outside necessarily, but those two options really help calm me when I need to chill out.

"As long as I'm on a roll here, let me also tell you that we babies love action. The things that you like to shake at us, well, they're more fun for you than they are for us. More than anything, we want to move! So anything you can do to help us in that pursuit would be greatly appreciated.

"We don't have very long spans of attention, so entertaining us is labor intensive, we know. Still, we love variety, we love to look at ourselves, and we love to finger paint in applesauce. Just wanted you to know. Applesauce is awesome."

Toddler Talk

So now that we've covered what a baby would like you to know, how about a toddler? Toddlers talk (boy, do they ever!), but lots of times we parents can't understand what they are trying to pass off as words. And even if we do understand them, it's hard to glean, based on their limited vocabularies, what they really want us to know. Let me try to translate some of it for you:

"So I get the feeling that you'd like to know what I'm thinking. Why did I pour the water out of the goldfish bowl and what happened to the fish? I dunno. Well, I know why I poured the water out, but I can't really explain it very well. I poured the water out because I really dig this cause-and-effect thing, and I wanted to see what would happen when I poured the water out. Unfortunately for me, the consequence was a whole lot of water on the floor and you showing me your mean face. Anyway, as for where the fish went...I'm afraid I don't have a conclusive answer for you on that one. I think he, um, swam away. Maybe under the front door and down the steps. He's looking for his friends. Yeah, that's it.

"Seriously, though, as a toddler, I can give you a little advice that you may not already know. If you want to keep us happy, try to anticipate what we're going to want before we want it. It's not that hard, really. We have a finite number of things we want. Food, entertainment, sleep, activity. If you get my lunch ready for me before I'm hungry, you will have a happy toddler. If you wash the sheets for my bed and my blankies too, and you put them back on my bed before I'm ready for my nap, you will have a happy toddler.

"And most importantly, if you let me have whatever toy I want, you will have a happy toddler. No, just kidding. You can't do that, because then I'd be a spoiled brat, but you can anticipate when I'm going to want a toy or a book, and be sure to bring things with you to entertain me. Let's say, for instance, when we go to a restaurant. It's boring waiting for my food, and um, I can't color yet! Doesn't anyone get that (a) toddlers can't really color, and (2) coloring is all we get to do? Offer me something else to do, and I will be happy. Bring a book to read to me while we're waiting for our food, bring me some crunchy snacks to munch on before my food arrives, and don't forget that I get thirsty. As a side note, *I* really couldn't care less how much noise I make or how much noise my toys make in public, but the people near you might care. And I just really don't feel like dealing with the disapproving looks. So try to bring along something to entertain me that is on the quiet side.

"If you're thinking that I am one demanding kid, well, you're right. Toddlers are demanding and self-centered. We're also cute as can be, which is a happy coincidence, because if we weren't so daggone cute, you wouldn't want to cater to us quite as much. Admit it. If you anticipate what I'm going to want, then we'll both live in peace and harmony. I will be calm and usually happy. How about you?"

Preschool Prattle

So if infants want periodic changes of scenery and a variety of activities, and toddlers want us to anticipate their needs, what do preschoolers want us to know? Let's have a listen:

"Preschoolers want to play. Period. Play, play, play. All we care about is playing—role playing, playing ball, playing house, playing games, playing anything and everything. We want to play because it's how we learn. Playing teaches us about cause and effect (a continuation of the toddler chronicles), it teaches us about sharing, communication, planning, prioritizing, and believe it or not, it gives us a sense of accomplishment. It also teaches us about social roles, power in a relationship, making and keeping friends, and transitioning from one activity to another.

"Did you realize all of that? No, I didn't think you did. All I know is that all preschoolers want to play and play hard. You don't need to worry too much about 'teachable moments' with us preschoolers, for we make our own. We learn from everything we do. We don't need workbooks, though we do enjoy learning about letters and numbers. One thing that preschoolers love is to feel like 'big kids.' We want to learn what the big kids learn. Still, we love to learn letters and numbers through play. Make it fun! Don't make us sit at a table and study. Everything can be a game. Remember that.

"So in conclusion, PLAY. Preschoolers want to play. That's what we want you to know."

In Grade School and Beyond…

The preschoolers want to play. Okay, we can do that. But what do the children want as they grow older? What about when they start kindergarten and beyond? Ironically, as children mature, their vocabularies develop at lightning speed, but we still struggle to understand them. Have we forgotten what we were like at ages five, eight, eleven, and beyond? Perhaps we have. Here's a bit of a refresher course:

"What do I want you to know? Everything! No, scratch that, I don't want you to know anything. So because of that, I think I'll tell you nothing. How's that for power? Okay, I'll drop the sass. Let me see if I can explain to you what I'd really like you to know.

"As I grow, I would like more than anything if you would walk beside me. I want to learn to handle the world on my own, but I just don't always feel ready. I don't want you to walk behind me and push, push, push, the way some parents do. I also don't want you to walk in front of me and protect me from everything the world might throw at me. I want to learn to handle things myself, and I want to feel you supporting me, as a friend.

"Yes, I know that you have to correct me sometimes, and that my sarcasm gets on your nerves, but I wish you'd understand that sass and sarcasm are my way of covering my insecurity. I want to be confident, but I'm not. And until I am, I have to pretend to be confident. Sass and sarcasm are my way of pretending to be confident. If you walk beside me, then I can do anything. If you're on my side, even if you're tough, then I can face whatever comes my way.

"I pretend that I don't care what you think, but I do. I pretend that whatever experiences you lived through in your youth are completely irrelevant to what I'm going through, but I do reflect on the stories you tell me. Walk beside me and tell me about the times that taught you how to be an adult. I want to be like you. I just don't want you to know that."

So There You Have It

At every stage of their lives, our children would love it if we already knew how to help them grow and learn. If we make a commitment to stay connected to our children, we have a far better chance of knowing what they need from us.

Before I wrote this chapter, I consulted my six-year-old daughter about what she would like me to know. I had to ask the question in a variety of ways before I got an answer that was truly responsive, but when I finally asked, "What should parents of six-year-olds always remember?" She said, "Just love us." Just love us. The simplicity of the answer speaks volumes, doesn't it? What do they really want us to know? Just love them.

Chapter Six:

"Mommy, Is Daddy Truthing?"

My daughter really said that to me one day. Her daddy is well known in our family as a smart aleck, and it takes significant practice to determine when he is telling the truth. I believe it's referred to as a "dry sense of humor." So the kids in the family especially have a hard time sometimes determining when he is telling the truth and when he is not.

We have talked to our daughter about lying, and how it's a bad thing to do, but she is at the age where she's trying to make sense of it all. It doesn't make sense to her that grown-ups sometimes think it's okay to lie, and sometimes they think it's the worst thing in the world. What's more, not all grown-ups consider the same things to be lies, and not everyone who lies is considered to be a "liar." Sometimes we don't even call them lies; we call them "stories," "fibs," and "bending the truth." Should we just scrap the whole system and stop lying to our children? About anything? This parent responds with a resounding "no!"

You may start out, when your child is a cute, snuggly, innocent babe-in-arms, promising yourself that you absolutely will not lie to your child. That may be a wonderful feeling for you during the first year or so of your child's life. It's wonderful to tell the truth to your child, but everything changes when they begin to talk. When they talk, they ask questions, and once that happens, you have reached a crossroads, my friend. Make no mistake, I believe in honesty. I am a scrupulous individual. But I am also a realist, and after having been both a teacher and a parent, I have learned the art of self-preservation.

Why do parents "stretch the truth" sometimes? Time. Sometimes you just don't have any. You need to move on through your day, and you can't do that if you're battling whining or tantrums. So every now and then, just to keep the peace, you opt to fib a little. Many of us have resorted to fibs such as these:

"I'm sorry, honey, we can't go through the drive-thru today, the restaurant is closed. They ran out of food."

"Gramps won't come to see you this afternoon until after you've taken a nap. He's going to call me in a little while and ask if you've taken a nap, and if you haven't, then he won't come over."

"You can't go to the playground today because it's the bugs' turn to use the slide today. The bugs and spiders get to use the playground equipment on certain days, and this just happens to be their day."

Shall I continue? No, you have the idea. Why do parents do this? From what I understand, they've been doing it for generations. Here's why: Parents need cooperation from their children to make it through the day or to simply progress to the next activity. We are not being cruel. We don't fib to hurt anyone. Quite the contrary, we are really just trying to keep the peace. Not only that, let's face it, sometimes we get desperate to move our children from Point A to Point B. Anticipating resistance from your child can create desperate times for parents. And you know what they say about desperate times...they call for the occasional fib.

Holiday Fibs

The Holiday Fib is one of my favorite types of fibs. The most famous of these, of course, is the Christmas One. The "Santa Claus lives at the North Pole with his elves and reindeer and once a year he flies around the world and delivers presents to girls and boys who have been good during the previous year" fib. We grown-ups have so much sadness and reality to live with every day that the way I see it, we perpetuate holiday fibs because we want to live in a fantasy world for a little while. If our children believe, then we can too, and for a few weeks at the end of every year, it's kind of nice to talk about flying reindeer and elves making toys and a round little man who loves everyone.

As for the other holiday fibs, they are perpetrated for the same reason as the Santa Fib, but not to the same degree. I remember when I was a little girl, my great-uncle explained to me that the Easter Bunny lives on the top of a mountain, where the trees are cut and there appears to be an area of open space. He didn't tell me the part about the trees being cut in those spaces to allow for power lines. To this day, when I look up at the mountains and see the cut-out space, I wonder if the Easter Bunny is busy coloring his eggs. I don't think of my great-uncle as a "liar," I think of him with fondness as a good storyteller.

It's always humorous when our children start to use those holiday fibs to their benefit. My daughter informed me not long ago that her playroom was a mess, and she believed that a leprechaun was responsible. I in turn informed her that the leprechaun who made the mess was long gone and unfortunately she would have to clean up the mess.

I don't mind the holiday fibs because they bring people joy. They bring joy to the adults who get to relive the stories with every child, and they bring joy to the children who get to believe. There are some parents who believe that holiday fibs are wrong and they try to change the minds of others, but for the most part, I think most people agree with me. I think Santa Claus, the Easter Bunny, and the many little leprechauns are safe for now.

Fibbing for Their Own Good

How do you know when it's okay to fib to your child? As with most other parenting issues, you follow instinct. But there is one time where it is absolutely, positively, always okay. If you need to fib a little to maintain or bolster a little one's self-esteem, then go right ahead. Here's how I figure it: There is a happy medium between constantly telling your child that she is the best child on the planet and never telling your child that she is the best child on the planet. If you think about your own childhood, you'll be able to identify where your parents were on this spectrum. Both extremes create their own problems, but a happy medium, somewhere in the middle, is the best place to be. I was once told that the most important thing we can do for our children is teach them the satisfaction in feeling proud of themselves.

Our parents—many of them, at least—did not concern themselves with self-esteem. It wasn't a concern when they were kids, and they found it indulgent to be concerned with our self-esteem. Not so, if you do it carefully. The key here is to fib as little as you can, let your child take the lead in identifying the "good" and the "bad," and be sure to talk about what can be improved. It doesn't help a child to constantly compliment him, nor does it help to be constantly critical. If you look at your preschooler's work and say, "I like all of the colors you used today," you are encouraging your child to try again. You have not said, "There is no young artist anywhere in the world that could compare to you," and you have not said, "What a piece of rubbish. Is that all you did at school today? Didn't you actually learn anything?"

In my mind, fibbing is okay if it is necessary to get your child thinking about his strengths. Fibbing is okay if you have a child who is extraordinarily hard on himself. Sometimes you have to fib to even out the extremes in your child's thinking. Just be careful. Tipping the scales too far could lead to arrogance or encourage a child to be satisfied with sub-par work. Your goal is for your child to feel that his work was a worthwhile experience and a good use of his time. Easy does it. Slow and steady. You'll be fine. Really.

The Most Important Times for "Truthing"

In general, I'm a proponent of fibbing to children if there's a good reason for it (and on holidays). If you need to fib to make it through the day or establish self-esteem, I'm all for it. There are times, though, when a parent must be honest with a child. No exceptions, no fibbing.

First, if there's going to be a change in your living situation or in your family, be honest. If you're going to move to a new home, if you and your partner are separating, or if a loved one has passed on, please tell the truth about it. These are some of the most difficult times to be truthful with children, but in my mind it is critical in your relationship with your child. One of our goals as parents is to establish trust with our children. As I've mentioned before, if they trust us, they will come to us later with the "big stuff." We need to tell children the truth about changes in their living situations because they are going to notice the changes! These little people are sharp—they are going to notice, and they are going to ask. If you fib to them, they will know.

The extent and depth of the explanation you give your child should depend on the child's age and maturity. Plan the explanation out ahead of time, try it out on someone if you need to make a practice run, pick a time that your child is ready to listen (not tired, hungry, angry, or frustrated), and talk to her quietly and calmly, using words that are on her level. If you sense that the talk is not going well, tell your child that you will continue it at another time. Then take some time to regroup. You may need to change the words or the approach, but continue to tell the truth. It is tempting to fib in these circumstances, because the reality is painful, awkward, or confusing, but these are times that you must be truthful.

Avoid the tendency to over-explain, however. Try not to re-visit the topic multiple times a day. Let your child drive the discussions if possible. If you feel that a conversation with your child about a life-changing event did not go well or needs more explanation, approach the topic (a) if your child brings it up, or (b) a few times a week, until you feel satisfied that you have explained the situation as best you can.

Another time that you must be truthful is if a child's schoolwork or behavior is consistently unacceptable. I told you that it's okay to fib a little to build self-esteem, and I still believe that, but there are times that call for nothing but the truth. A friend of mine decided to move her child to another school because she was not satisfied with how the teacher was managing her child's outbursts. My friend chose to tell her child that the outbursts were part of the problem, that they were unacceptable and would have to be addressed, and that she didn't feel that the teacher was the best person to help. When I asked her why she chose to tell her child about the reasons for the change rather than just telling her child that she would be moving to a "bigger, better school," this is what she said: "I knew that she was smart enough to know that the outbursts and the teacher had something to do with the change of schools. I thought she should see that her behavior really did play a part in the decision."

Not all parents would make the same choice, but I would. I think she handled it beautifully. The change in schools did not end the behavioral problems completely—it was not a solution in and of itself—but it was a positive step in the process, which opened up the discussion of her behavior with her daughter. My friend told me that it seemed as if her daughter appreciated the fact that she had been kept informed and treated with respect.

Recently I had a conversation with a father who said that he was always honest with his child when he had to be away from home. He travels often because of his job, and he always tells his child when he will be away and, just as importantly, when he will be home. He tells his child when he will leave, where he is going, and what special activity they can both look forward to when he gets home. He also tries to talk to his child every evening while he is away. His little one feels a sense of stability, even when he is gone, because he has been honest. He said to me, "I am not the perfect parent. Not even close. But this is one thing that I know I can do."

The truth is a funny thing. Sometimes it helps you, and sometimes it doesn't. Please, please don't interpret this chapter to mean that I am a proponent of lying, period. I'm not. I fully support fibbing that does not hurt anyone if you occasionally need to use it to gain cooperation, to play along with the holiday myths, or to build a little self-esteem. But children appreciate the truth, and they learn by example, so my suggestion is to use fibbing sparingly. I like to think of fibbing like a spice—it can help, but a little goes a long way.

Chapter Seven:

Humor in the House

There is humor in parenthood, if you are open to seeing it. The first thing you can do to be sure that there is humor in your house is to laugh at yourself. If you've never done that, give it a try. It keeps us humble to laugh at ourselves. If you're like me, major things don't usually go wrong in your life, but enough little things go wrong to seriously frustrate you sometimes. Fortunately I grew up learning to laugh at myself, and I am determined to make my home one that is filled with laughter.

I know a mother named Karen who has a wonderful sense of humor. She has not had an easy life in the past, and she doesn't have it easy now. But she laughs. At herself, at others, at life in general. I asked her how she developed such a great sense of humor, and she told me that she had an aunt and uncle who modeled humor for her whenever she was around them, which, fortunately for her, was a lot.

You're Being Watched, Part II

In every aspect of your life as a parent, your child is watching you to see how you will handle the situation. It doesn't even matter what the situation is, you're being watched to see how you will handle it. In my opinion, children begin to learn humor at a very early age. The first type of humor they learn is "silliness." What a baby finds funny is exaggerated movement, including funny faces and dancing. At age ten months, our daughter could boogie in her swing. She had a beat, I tell you.

The first thing you should know about babies and humor is that you can diffuse some of that tension you feel over being a parent by entertaining your child. Get silly. Stick out that derriere and shake it! Small children don't mind if you're not a good dancer or you have more "junk in the trunk" than you would like. They love it! And the best part is...you are teaching your child that the two of you can have fun together, can laugh together. That's lesson #1, folks. Lesson #2 is...do it again. Use it as an exercise session, a stress reducing technique, and a humor teaching tool. Who knew that boogie-ing could accomplish so much?

After the baby stage, the next thing your child learns about humor is that it's funny when things just don't look right. They're turned the wrong way or again they're exaggerated in some way. When my sister was a toddler, my mom decided to play a little practical joke on her. She tied a full-sized orange to a tiny tree in our front yard. The little baby tree could hardly hold the weight of the orange, but somehow it managed. My mom pointed out to my sister that the tree had grown an orange overnight, and my sister proceeded to study the orange hanging on the tree with unparalleled interest. Watching her daughter study that orange hanging on the tree struck my mom as funny, and when she laughed, my sister laughed too. Why did my sister laugh? Because her mother was laughing!

Then Mom explained to my sister that it was silly for a tiny tree like that to grow such a big orange. She explained that she had tied the orange on the tree and it was called a joke. It was silly.

It's not often that we consider teaching humor to our children, but maybe we should. We should teach them early what things are funny and what things are not. What does it mean to play a little trick on someone without taking things too far? Watch the kids' shows on television with them and point out what's silly. Ask your child, "Why do you think that person is laughing? What's funny?" Teaching humor is the same as teaching anything else to our kids: it involves modeling and practice, and it builds on itself.

As if you don't have enough to teach, right? Now I'm asking you to teach humor too. Here's why: we need to teach humor because we need to monitor the type of humor that our children learn and how they interpret what they see. It's okay to giggle a little at the slapstick humor of cartoons, but what if your child thinks it's funny when someone falls in a store because it looks similar to a fall he has seen on TV? You need to teach humor so you can help differentiate between slapstick humor and an unfortunate accident.

You can model humor by explaining to your child the things that you do that are silly, and you can call yourself names like "silly" or "forgetful" or even "a ninny" for doing them. But you need to be on deck also when it's time to teach your little one that we don't call other people those names, even if they do silly things. Name calling is never humor, and some parents don't get that. Kids don't engage in name calling unless they have seen it done somewhere. Hmmmm... Where could that be?

Teaching humor means modeling your sense of humor in an age-appropriate way to a child who is trying to grasp the nuances of what is funny and what is not. Children understand silliness at an early age, simple jokes as preschoolers, jokes with punch lines as they enter elementary school, and sarcasm much later. We can gently guide them into a great sense of humor if we teach them to laugh at their own mistakes, but never at the misfortune of others.

I propose the following guidelines (the don'ts):

1. Teasing and bullying are not funny.
2. We never make jokes that make other people feel bad about themselves.
3. It is never funny to harm living creatures or property.

Other than those three "don'ts," teach humor as you would anything else. Start slow, model humor, laugh at yourself, laugh with your children, and have a good time. Putting humor in your house means that it will become a part of your life and your children's lives.

I was taught humor at a young age and have valued it ever since. To have someone tell you that your smile lights up a room or that you are fun to be around is priceless. When you teach your children humor, you are giving them the most unique gift they will ever receive. They'll never outgrow it and will treasure it forever.

Chapter Eight:
Where's the Wisdom?

Before you had children, did you say to yourself, "I don't have to worry. When I don't know how to handle a situation, I'll just ask Grandma. She'll know what to do." Or if not Grandma, then maybe you substituted another beloved relative or friend's name. That's how new parents get through the pre-child jitters. We tell ourselves, "People have been doing this for thousands of years. It can't be that hard. We'll be fine."

Well, it's true. People have been adding children to their families for thousands of years, and you *will* be fine. It's that middle statement that gives me pause: "It can't be that hard." Hmmmm. Yes, it can be hard, and if you're like every other parent, you'll think that it's only hard for you. That's what I thought, until one of my friends set me straight. This particular lady is the wonderful mother of three beautiful children (really, I mean it), and she has regularly babysat for other children too. She is poised, articulate, clever, artsy, and above all, competent. And I still like her! Seriously, though, she has set me straight several times on this whole parenting thing, and I am thankful for her wisdom.

On more than one occasion, I have brought my daughter to my friend's house for babysitting and have nearly collapsed on her sofa from pure frustration and exhaustion. I met this lady when she was my student in a college-level business law course. When she and I met, I was the teacher and she was the student. In 2006, when I became a mom, though, our roles reversed. She became the teacher. Her oldest daughter was four when my husband and I became parents. She babysat children who were anywhere from infants to pre-teens. She has seen a lot of parenting approaches, and she, along with her husband, has done a lot of parenting too.

Every so often, I have planted myself on my friend's sofa and have given her the "woe is me" chapter of the day. I have detailed every one of my daughter's misdeeds and ornery episodes. I have told her what my daughter did, what I did, and what my husband didn't do. I poured out my feelings of inadequacy as a parent and asked her what I should do. The thing is I'm not sure if I was asking for her advice or asking her to tell me that I was not alone in this adventure. This journey. This quagmire.

And then one day she said to me, kindly, "You're no different than anyone else. The same conversations go on in every household. We all get tired. We all lose our tempers. We all yell. It happens to all of us." There it was. What I needed to hear. It's nothing earth-shattering, but it is mind-altering. She simply gave me the reassurance that I am normal. That our household is normal.

We're normal. As parents, we all have variations of the same problems. Some of us have trouble keeping our child in the "time out" chair. Some of us have children who cry when we leave them. Some of us have children who would rather sleep anywhere other than in their own beds. Some of us have children who are bold enough to ask a man who is exiting a pool wearing a Speedo, "Where is the rest of your bathing suit?" Any parent who has a bit of experience eventually realizes that we all work through shades of the same issues. We also learn not to judge other parents too harshly, for we never know what is just around the corner in our own world of parenting.

The Wisdom We Seek

For some odd reason, before my daughter joined our family, I thought that I could learn all I needed to know from one book and one person. I was trying to simplify. I quickly learned, however, that it isn't one book or one person who has all the answers. And, more importantly, the wisdom you find one day may be all you needed and more, but the next day, parenthood could very well dump a new "issue" on your doorstep. The source of the wisdom from yesterday has nothing to say on today's topic.

We cannot derive all of our parenting information or guidance from one or two sources. Not if we want to find truly helpful suggestions or be comforted and reassured. It takes a whole host of sources to do that. Every experience you have, every book you read, every person you talk to will bring you some bit of wisdom. Some you discard, some are good ideas but just aren't "you," and some you decide to try.

Two ideas that I highly recommend trying are these: frozen waffles for teething babies and covering your table with the sticky-edged plastic wrap before undertaking an art project. (Note: For the frozen waffle idea, it is the BABY who chews on the waffle, not you. And supervise carefully to avoid a choking hazard.)

We need a variety of sources to consult because no one book or person can provide us with everything we will need. Let's face it: parenting is often about managing the details, troubleshooting tiny problems before they become big ones, summarizing, and prioritizing. We all do these differently, and we all need practice in different areas.

So where's the wisdom? Everywhere. While I was conducting research for this book, I asked many people, and many of them strangers, questions like these: "What did you do best as a parent?" "What would you do differently if you were starting over?" "What's the most important thing that parents should teach their children?" The answers I got were truly enlightening. Most of them centered around teaching children respect—for their elders, for their teachers, for their peers, and for themselves. It was heartening to learn that there are still people in this country who value respect, thoughtfulness, consideration for others...you know, the old-fashioned values. I like that.

I wrote this section on finding the wisdom because it is so important that we parents realize that the wisdom we need to help us with the daily struggles of parenting exist all around us. Most people have either had parents or *are* parents. We all have a little experience.

If there are so many parents around, then why is parenting such an isolating experience at times? Maybe it isn't for everyone, but it has been for me. Our culture, unfortunately, programs us to announce our successes to the world but to hide our challenges. Most parents at the playground are not willing to turn to another parent and say, "Yeah, I don't really know what I'm doing as a parent. I'm winging it. I'll try my best, but beyond that, I have no idea how this kid's going to turn out."

Next time you're at the playground (or the library or the mall or the grocery store), look around you at the other parents and imagine how great it would be if we all just admitted that we're hanging on by a thread and we're just hoping to make it till tomorrow. It would be great, but it's not likely to happen.

I take pride in being the one who says it first. It's not so much that I enjoy looking like a buffoon, but I find that I learn a whole lot more when I admit that I could use someone else's opinion. Try it sometime. When you confess your insecurities, it can be amazing to see the support and camaraderie that follows. You might even make a new friend.

Children are one of life's great equalizers. Regardless of whether you are highly educated, not educated, rich, poor, purple, orange, or polka-dotted, if you have kids, you have issues. We all struggle with our children about something. Don't look past people who might offer you some insight. You don't have to ask advice from only members of your socio-economic group or from parents who are your same age. Senior citizens are a wealth of information about parenting—they have great stories, and they have a way of making you feel things are going to be okay. If you want to learn to be a better parent, talk to people. Ask them things. You are likely to be amazed at what you learn.

Here's an example: Not long after our daughter came to us, it was a beautiful fall day, and I thought it would be a perfect occasion for a mother-daughter trip to a large toy store. I had gone to this store many times by myself, but this was the first time I would be sharing the experience with my daughter. I envisioned myself handing her one toy after another, letting her play with them for a few minutes, and reveling in her glee to have so many toys to look at and enjoy. Did it work out that way? Read on.

I don't know what happened to my little girl when we got into that store. It was like someone had cast a spell on my delightful little baby and turned her into a shrieking howler monkey. She wanted every single toy off of every shelf to be in her hands, and she DID NOT want to give any of them back. Her shrieking reverberated through the rafters, and I tried everything I could think of to make it stop. Except leave the store. It didn't even occur to me to leave the store! I am nothing if not determined, and I think that I was subconsciously determined to make this outing what I had dreamt it would be.

So after ten minutes or so of the mayhem, a lady who looked like she might be fifteen or so years older than me dared to walk down the same aisle that I was inhabiting with my cart and my howler monkey. She seemed fairly unaffected by the fussing, whining, and crying, and she even gave me a little smile. It was a kind smile, one of those that says, "I know what you're going through, dear." So I turned to her and said, in a bewildered voice, "I thought this was going to be fun. It's her first trip to a toy store, and I really thought it would be fun."

She said, with an even bigger smile, "Oh, no, it's not about what the mother thinks will be fun. It has switched now to what the child thinks will be fun."

Now why didn't I think of that? It's not a complicated concept. Of course a baby is going to want everything in the store. What made me think that my child would be any different than any other baby?

The wisdom that I gleaned from my brief encounter with the smiling lady in the toy store is that I didn't think it through because my mind stopped at my own fantasy of what the experience would be. I thought it would be a beautiful bonding experience for us, and my vision of playing with my baby in the toy store blocked out my understanding of what babies are like when toys are around. The smiling lady was right. I didn't get to call the shots anymore—where fun is concerned, at least. Once I had a child, she got to decide what fun was, and my fantasies of love and laughter in the toy store are...long gone.

Don't feel sad for me, though, because I did gain something that day. I gained the wisdom of a lady who had clearly been through this type of experience. I didn't bond with my daughter on that particular outing, but I did bond with a smiling lady who made me feel as if I wasn't the only mother whose child morphed into a shrieking howler monkey on the way into the toy store. I believe this feeling I experienced with the smiling lady is called "camaraderie." It was nice. I liked it.

Back to the Books

Nobody loves books more than I do. I treasure them. If I need to learn about something, I always turn to the written word. But the written word, at least about parenting, can be confusing. My advice on reading about parenting is this: Do it in moderation. Read until you have a general sense of what your child should do at what age and what you should watch for where illness and developmental delays are concerned. Notice that I said *a general sense*. Don't consult the books every day as you watch to see what your child is doing on the fourteenth day of the thirteenth month of her life. You will drive yourself crazy.

I've heard more than one physician say that parents worry too much about when their children will be potty trained. The "how-to" parenting books have parents so worked up that they are fixated on things that tend to work themselves out. I've heard a physician say, "It's highly likely that a child will be potty trained before he or she goes off to college."

It isn't just potty training that we parents worry about, though. It's everything. If you spend much time reading the "how-to" parenting books, beware. Beware of the feeling that you are not doing anything right. Beware of feeling that your child does not fit into any of the categories and therefore must be some sort of deviant. Beware of feeling that you didn't get what you were looking for in that book so you must go buy another book.

There is absolutely nothing wrong with wanting to educate yourself—that's being a responsible parent. What I'm saying is that you must vary your sources of wisdom. Don't just go to the books. I am a huge proponent of learning by observation. People watching. Learn from the books, but then put the knowledge to use by talking to parents, grandparents, teachers, and anyone else who might shed some light on your situation. And by all means listen to your child.

Even before a child can talk, she can provide you with information. As I suggested in the earlier chapters of this book, use your power of observation to see what doesn't work, what does work, and what your parental intuition is telling you. If your child can talk, then listen. Children can teach you a lot about parenting if you take the time to decipher their special code. Use all of your senses to gather wisdom, search it out of unlikely sources, and observe the heck out of the world around you. Where's the wisdom? Everywhere.

Chapter Nine:

Traditional or Trendy?

I am not a trendy-type person. I did not grow up in a trendy atmosphere. Conservative was the name of the game in my parents' home. We followed traditions, we did not break rules, and we learned proper etiquette. I am actually quite proud of those things, really, but one thing that amuses me about myself is that I have inherited my mother's steadfast loyalty to *the centerpiece.*

My mother did not serve a meal to guests— ever—without a proper centerpiece. She arranged fresh flowers herself and she set a beautiful table. She learned from her aunt, and I learned from her, that a hostess should make her guests feel special, and a centerpiece shows that the hostess put care and planning into the occasion. Perhaps I don't utilize the chafing dishes or the crystal bowls that my mother and my aunt did, but I am nevertheless a believer in the centerpiece. Particularly at holiday gatherings, when my mother would be present at the table, I put a lot of thought into the centerpiece.

One holiday season, several weeks before Christmas, I sat at my place at the kitchen table, alone, enjoying a bit of solitude. I looked at the fireplace in our kitchen and admired the Christmas décor above and beside it. I admired the tree that we had added to the kitchen just the day before. I admired so many things about our holiday preparations. And then I looked at the table. At the moment I looked, the table was partially covered by a plastic tablecloth, not for aesthetic purposes, but because my daughter had been playing with Play-Doh that morning, and I try to corral the tiny little slivers of Play-Doh that get away onto the plastic tablecloth. When I was a child, playing with Play-Doh consisted of opening the cans and proceeding to squish and mold, squish and mold. Nowadays there are so many accessories available to a Play-Doh aficionado. And not surprisingly, in the middle of our kitchen table sat a decent representation of most of the Play-Doh accessory collection.

As I sat there ruminating on what sort of centerpiece I should use for this year's holiday meal, I thought to myself, *Maybe I should leave all the Play-Doh stuff here, and let our daughter create the centerpiece.* When I told her about my idea, she loved it! She created a bowl-vase in a lovely hue of taupe (you know, that color you get when all of the Play-Doh colors get mixed together). I put some fresh flowers inside, and we went with it. A Play-Doh centerpiece. A foundation of "traditional" with touches of modern thrown in. That's what I believe in for life, for tablescapes, and most especially for parenting.

Considering the "Traditional"

Traditional theories of child rearing have something to be said for them. If you are selective, there are some that have real merit. For example, the "old wisdom" of traditional parenting stresses the importance of children learning to be self-sufficient. Children of generations past learned that a household operates when everyone helps with the chores. I am not talking child labor here. Of course not. What I am saying is that children in past generations had responsibilities, and I am all for that. Children's responsibilities should be age appropriate, but children need to learn that work comes before play.

A friend of mine in college once told me what it was like to grow up in a traditional Italian family. She told me that, in her family, when a young girl turned six, she was expected to help in the kitchen at big family gatherings. She said, "A little girl is given a step-stool, she pushes it up to the sink, and she washes those huge pots that are used to cook pasta. And if they aren't clean when she's finished, she does it again!" My friend had fond memories of being included in the "women's club" that took over the kitchen at a family gathering. She didn't see it as drudgery, she saw it as a sign that she was contributing to the family's meal.

In generations past, the children had to help, in the home, in the fields, wherever the family was. It was out of necessity that children were given chores. Today it's still out of necessity that children should be assigned chores. Not only because we parents need help (we do!), but because it teaches children to be self-sufficient. That, in turn, builds their self-esteem, and they see that they can contribute to the family. Let's face it, the children of today are spoiled, and it is necessary to balance that spoiling with a sense of responsibility.

I've always said about myself that I am spoiled, but I am not a spoiled brat. That's also what I hope my daughter will be—spoiled, without being a brat. Almost all American children are spoiled in one way or another—it's nearly inevitable. But despite being spoiled, our children should see that they can be givers as well as takers. It's a win-win situation: we get help with the hundreds of chores that need to be done every week, and our children learn to value their contribution to their household.

So what else did "traditional" parents do that we can use? Should we apply brandy to the gums of a teething infant? Uh, no. Should we give our children enemas when they have a cold? Definitely not. Should we show them the error of their ways using a belt, behind the barn? I don't have a barn, but even if I did...no. Should we teach them to respect their elders? Absolutely. But how?

I love to listen to my dad talk about his childhood. The thing that always strikes me when he talks about his childhood is the fondness with which he speaks of his grandparents. His grandfather was especially important to him. It was not because of his grandfather's career (he was a dairy farmer), it was not because of his esteemed educational background (he had very little), it was not because of his wealth (again, very little), but it was because my great-grandfather loved my dad, and they spent time together every day. My dad and his grandfather were friends, and that made all the difference.

In fact, I have always found it interesting that my dad called his grandfather by his given name, "Charlie." Not "Grandpa" or "Granddad" or any of the other terms of endearment that we choose for our grandfathers. Charlie was a lover of music and taught my dad how to play the saxophone, which he has played ever since.

Charlie not only taught my dad how to read music, he also taught him how to read books. He once told my dad, "If you're reading and you don't know a word, don't fret. Just say 'wheelbarrow' and keep on going." They laughed about it and kept going.

I recently told that story to my daughter, and she loved the approach. I told her that she shouldn't do that at school when she's reading for her teacher, but at home, when we're practicing, it makes us laugh. What a gift. What a simple, silly gift to pass down from one generation to another. When you're learning and you're not sure of yourself, just say "wheelbarrow" and keep on going.

My great-grandfather knew the secret of how to earn the respect of a child. He knew that the most important thing to a child, and the way to earn a child's respect, was to give that child the gift of undivided attention. There is no substitute for time spent with a child. Despite the fact that my dad called his grandfather by his first name, the pure nature of their relationship demonstrated a respect that went both ways. And to this day, the two things that are perhaps most precious to my dad are his music and his books. In my opinion, my dad's love of music and books are his greatest legacy, because he, in turn, passed them on to me.

Spending quality time with the treasured children in your life is not only *a* value, it is *of* value. Children of today try to make us believe that their love can be bought, and some adults are suckered into believing such a fallacy, but in the long run it isn't true. Buying a child's love is a short-term fix; it only lasts until the child's next materialistic "need" comes along. But spending time with children, and especially laughing with children, is priceless. Though it is traditional wisdom and has been said many times, it always bears repeating: time spent with children is never wasted.

Sometimes it seems that the world we live in is so different from fifty or a hundred years ago that it can't possibly be relevant anymore. Not so. Traditional parenting stressed the premium values of loyalty, conscientiousness, and good manners. Children in past generations were taught values that helped them succeed in their lives.

Ask yourself, "What values do I think are the most important? What values do I want my child to learn from me?" I chose *loyalty, conscientiousness,* and *good manners* because they are especially important to me, but I recognize that the values that others name may be different. (And by the way, despite my light-hearted discussion earlier in the book about "fibbing," I do indeed value honesty.)

How do we teach our children traditional values? We model them. As you spend time with a child, you come upon situations and encounters with other people whereby you model your own values. Then you discuss with your child how each person acted, why they acted a certain way, and what you feel is the proper way to handle a situation such as that one.

There are wonderful children's books that present values in terms that children understand. My daughter has a library full of "values-based" books. Mr. Guinea Pig learns table manners. Mrs. Jack Rabbit learns to overcome jealousy. Johnny Junebug learns to share his toys. Abigail Ant learns to say she's sorry. But still...there's no substitute for a child seeing values modeled in real life, and that means, once again, that our parents and grandparents did know a thing or two about parenting. They didn't just send us to school and let the teaching stop there.

Traditional parenting was about one-on-one teaching. No, it wasn't always perfect. Traditional parents were not always perfect. But that doesn't mean that we can't learn from them. Traditional parenting does have a place in today's world. It is the smart parents who look to the past for guidance as they work with their children to shape the future.

And Now For the "Trendy"...

My daughter has been invited to several parties since she began school. The parties were hosted by lovely families, and the invitations were works of art. They were clever and artistic. (I believe there was glitter involved.) The aspect of the invitations that I found amusing, nay, confusing, was the statement, printed neatly at the bottom of the invitation, "Parents are welcome to stay."

Have you seen this? I hadn't. It threw me into quite a tizzy. What does that statement mean? Am I supposed to stay? Do they think that my child is going to be so poorly behaved that they need back-up? Do they think that the parents will feel left out if they are not invited too? Should I call and ask if they *want* me to stay? WHAT SHOULD I DO?

I ended up calling to ask if they wanted me to stay, and I came away from those conversations wholly unsatisfied: "It's up to you. It's personal preference." In the effort to be accommodating these days, so many people are saying to each other, "It's personal preference." It's not that I don't appreciate the thought, but saying to an unsure parent, "It's personal preference" does not help the unsure parent! One of the trends that I see today, in parenting as well as other areas, is that expectations are unclear, and everywhere we turn, it's "personal preference."

When I was a child, we were invited to a party, we went, we ate cake and ice cream, we played, and that was it. Parents dropped us off at the beginning of the party and collected us when it was over. Isn't the purpose of having a party—to provide two hours of free babysitting for other parents? No? Oh, I thought it was.

The "Parents are Welcome to Stay" phenomenon comes from kindness in the hearts of parents who place it on the invitation. It is a thoughtful thing to do. I guess. But I think that we need to raise our children so they don't need us to stay with them at a party. We should teach them the manners that they need to be lovely guests at a party. We should not have to stay with them at a party to be sure that they're doing okay. And we should not coddle our children so much that they can't exist without us.

What troubles me in our society today is that I see parents who are not clear in their expectations. They are not clear in their directions to their children (or in their party invitations!). I have heard so many parents talk and talk and talk and talk to their children, and then the children ask the same question that began all the talking. Why is this? Because the question asked by the child needed a "yes" or "no" answer. Parents are leery of saying "no," so they try to cover that by talking up a storm.

When you hear yourself say more than two sentences to your child when you are answering a question, say to yourself, "too many words." We live in a world of too many words. Children cannot absorb as many words as are hurled at them every day. I call this trend "Too many words, not enough clarity."

We need to work harder to be clear in our expectations. If you need time to formulate an answer with only a few words, tell your child, "Please wait for a moment. I'm thinking of a way to explain my answer to you." Today's parents are made to feel that they must do everything for their children immediately, including respond to them. Our children are demanding and impatient, partly because we live in a fast-moving world and partly because we permit them to be. We do not have to answer them immediately, and more times than not, it's far more effective to take some time to formulate a concise answer than to answer right away and provide a "sloppy" answer.

Not only are our kids confused when they are given too many words and not enough clarity, we are also! When a lack of clarity extends into our lives so far that it even extends to party invitations, I say it's time to revolt. It's hard enough when we have to struggle each and every day to phrase our directions to our children clearly enough that they can follow them, but when we are confused by a simple little party invitation, then things have gone too far. This world of "personal preference" that we live in has made our lives too complicated.

So how do you fight a lack of clarity from adults? You politely ask for clarification and you don't back down until you get it. Don't suffer in silence wondering what should be done. Ask the hostess, the teacher, the coach, or whoever else is in a position to give guidance. And please don't accept "It's personal preference" as an answer.

Really, it isn't just our children who need clear directions and expectations. We parents do too. So my solution to the "Parents are Welcome to Stay" movement of today (otherwise known as the "Too Many Words, not Enough Clarity" trend) is to start a grass roots movement. Where you see ambiguity in the world, particularly in the world of parenting, ask for guidance. Ask for clarity. "I'm not clear on this. Could you give me your opinion?" "If you were making this decision, what would you do?" "I want to be as clear as possible on this topic. What do you make of this?"

Another Bit of "Trendy"

Another trend in parenting that is running rampant is the "Elevating the Child to Adult Status" movement. Several years ago, I was shopping in a crowded mall when I couldn't help but notice a father trying to calm his tearful yet tyrannical daughter. He led her over to a spot where they wouldn't be trampled and said to her, on bended knee, "I need you to help me work this out. We need to find a logical and reasonable solution to this disagreement. I know that if we talk about it, we can come to a mutual understanding." Whoa, dude! Are you kidding me with this? The child was no more than six years old!

First of all, w-a-a-a-y too many words! Second of all, no child who is crying in a mall is interested in being logical or reasonable. Thirdly, she didn't want a "mutual understanding," she wanted a toy! This father gets points in my book for trying. Seriously, many fathers wouldn't even take their daughter to a mall, let alone attempt to calmly deal with a meltdown. But his plan went awry when he spoke to her as if she was his equal. Again, I know there are parents out there who would disagree with me, but being as this is my book, I shall continue.

Our children are not our peers. We are not equals. As I tell my daughter, "When you are grown and you move to your own home and have your own family, you will be the boss, but until then, your dad and I are the bosses here. You are not." Now, having said that, I believe both children and parents deserve to be treated with respect, with a minimum of yelling, and with a maximum use of good manners. Just because I say that we are not equals does not mean that I feel that children should be treated as though their feelings don't matter. But when parents elevate their children to adult status, they are giving away their authority. A successful relationship between a parent and child requires an understanding of trust, respect, and who holds the power in the relationship. (Plus, you have waited so long to be the boss—don't give the power away now that you have some!)

Why do parents elevate their children to the status of adults? I have several theories on that one. First, it's possible that the parent never created a parent-child relationship early on and doesn't know how to do it now. An adult-type relationship may be the parent's only hope of having a relationship at all. Another theory is that the parent loves the child, the child is mature and seems competent to understand adult problems, and the parent needs a friend.

We live in a society where family dynamics are complicated, work is complicated, school is complicated, and sometimes it is easy to turn to a child for support. The problem is that children, no matter how mature they seem, are not prepared to process adult problems. They cannot and should not shoulder such a burden. Children pretend that they can be adult-like and "handle" an adult-like relationship, but all the while they are hiding the pain that it causes.

Aside from that, children who are elevated to adult status eventually use that relationship to try to gain the upper hand. Translated: They use their power to try to get stuff. The "stuff" can be material things or privileges. Elevating children to the status of adults is a dangerous thing to do. It works in the short term, but in the long term it erodes the respect that a child should hold for his or her parent.

So Which is Better? Traditional or Trendy?

The answer is: They both have their place. How about a peaceful coexistence between traditional and trendy? To begin with, parents who believe in giving their children choices are doing the right thing. Limited choices are healthy for children, from choosing their socks to choosing which vegetable to eat. (A smart parent lets a child make a choice when the choice itself doesn't really matter.)

A mother I know started when her daughter was very young to help her make good choices. When she was little, the mother helped her choose outfits that matched. As the daughter grew, the mother helped her choose which science fair project would work for her, and as she entered adulthood, the mother listened as she debated the pros and cons of various careers. The mother was truly touched one day when her daughter turned to her in the midst of a discussion and said, "Mom, thanks for giving me a brain." Translated, the mother and I believe that she meant, "Thanks, Mom, for teaching me how to make good choices."

The only way to teach children how to make good choices is to allow them to practice. The trend that I call "limited choices" is one that works. Give a child enough choices to give the child a sense of empowerment, but not so many that it causes confusion. And equally as important, allow the child to make a poor choice every now and then in order to experience what happens as a result of a poor choice. Standing back and watching while your child makes a bad decision is excruciatingly painful. It's so painful that I believe most parents are not able to do it. Most parents, some of the best I know, have always rescued their children from undesirable consequences. What does that teach a child? Nothing.

Our job as parents is to teach our children how to survive in a world that is full of choices. If you start your children making choices early and allow their choices to become more advanced as they grow older, they will gain confidence in their ability to make good choices. If children get plenty of practice making choices, they will trust themselves to make the right ones. If they can do that, then we have done our jobs as parents.

In addition to the "Limited Choices" trend, I also applaud the "Follow Your Bliss" trend. This one applies as a child's talents begin to emerge. When I was a kid, kids took piano lessons. Period. I don't know of any kids who were given a choice in the matter. Some of us were competent pianists, others showed no competency whatsoever, but we were not allowed to quit until sometime during junior high school, when our parents were so worn down from our pleading that they couldn't take it anymore.

I don't hear of that happening so much anymore. There are so many activities to pick from now—everything from tae kwon do to poetry writing. Little girls can now join cheerleading squads and children can become junior politicians. Because there is no way that a child can do it all, I see parents waiting and watching a bit more than they did even ten years ago. Wait to see what your children show an interest in doing, what they show talent for doing, and *then* get them involved in it. Not long ago, the trend was for parents to sign their children up for anything and everything. Again, too many choices, too much confusion.

Children should pursue, as hobbies, what interests them. They should pursue what interests *them*, not what we always wanted to do and didn't. I did not coin the phrase "follow your bliss," but I have seen it many places and believe in it with all of my heart.

My daughter is so into horses, ponies, and all things equestrian these days. Where did she get it from? My husband and I don't know. We're city kids. The only time I rode a horse, I was thrown, and I never did "get back on." I don't think my husband has ever been on a horse. So where did our daughter develop this love of horses? That's one of life's mysteries that is fun to watch because it unfolds before our eyes, and it shows us that our little one is becoming a person, independent of us, with her own preferences, hobbies, and "bliss."

I am admittedly a control freak, but I believe that we have to give our children some opportunities to call the shots. Otherwise they won't have their own personalities and won't be able to make choices when the time comes for them to (gasp!) grow up. And it isn't just that they need to be able to make decisions; they need to have confidence and trust their decisions. They won't be able to do that if we don't let them give it a try every once in a while. Keep in mind here, however, that I believe in limited choices. Everything these days seems to be taken too far at times, and on the other end of the spectrum are the kids who decide everything.

One mother I heard about recently allowed her children to sit ON the table while eating because she was afraid that if she told them to sit in a chair, they wouldn't like her. I will tell you with 100 percent certainty that, as a mother and as a teacher, I am quite strict. But children can recognize the difference between a mean parent and a strict parent. When a parent is mean, there is no love, but when a parent is strict, there is only love. The next chapter provides you with a plan for how to be a strict parent, full of love but determined to raise a nicely behaved child.

Chapter Ten:

The Privileges System for Children

There are many theories and systems out there that detail how to manage your child. They promise quick results and happy children. This is one of those systems. I developed this system in 2008 after reading many books about managing children's behavior. This system utilizes ideas that you may have heard before and combines them to create a plan, a "game," if you will. My job here is to provide the plan. Your job is to bring the determination to follow through with the plan. If you do, it will change the decibel level in your house and shape your children's behavior, with quick results. It takes dedication, but it *does* work. I know, because I have used this system with my own daughter and taught this system to other parents who have used it successfully.

Here is a brief overview of the system:

a. Say to your child, "Wouldn't it be great if Mom and Dad didn't yell anymore, and you got to do what you wanted to do?"

b. Identify with your child what privileges he or she enjoys. Explain that a "privilege" is "something special that you get to do." (More about privileges later.)

c. You write (or draw) one privilege on each of five sticky notes. Display the privileges in a place where everyone in the house can see them.

d. Explain to your child that the "game" is played like this: The child should enjoy the privileges as he or she normally would, but if you see unacceptable behavior throughout the day and evening, you will count. If you reach the count of three, a privilege will be "counted out" or "lost." At that point, you remove the sticky note from where it is displayed and place it out of sight. And once a privilege has been enjoyed, you remove that sticky note from sight too.

e. As the day and evening progresses, your child will enjoy some privileges and possibly lose other privileges. Very quickly your child will realize that unacceptable behavior leads to loss of privileges and acceptable behavior leads to enjoyment of privileges.

Keep in mind that this system will develop and evolve over time. I will attempt to answer the questions that are in your mind, and I will give you scripts to use with your child, but after you master how the "game" is played, you will have to make adjustments based on your child, your schedule, and a myriad of other factors. The good news is that this is a system that you can use to manage your child's behavior until he or she grows up and leaves your home. The privileges will change, but that's an easy change to make if you have the rest of the system in place.

Also, a number of parents have asked me at what age I think a child can begin to understand the idea of privileges. I used the word "privilege" with my daughter beginning at age eighteen months. I am a believer that you can introduce words to a toddler even though they may not fully comprehend them right away. Over time, used in context, my daughter came to under-stand that privileges are "fun things that you get to do." (P.S. Wait until you hear the many ways that the word "privilege" can be pronounced by a little one.) I began the Privileges System in earnest when my daughter was slightly past three years old. She couldn't read, so we drew a picture of each privilege on each sticky note.

The naysayers among you will claim that a child that young cannot understand this system. I disagree. It's a simple system, and the sticky notes help children see their privileges. I contend that if you wait until a child is five or older, your job will be infinitely more difficult. Most parents don't realize that the toddler and preschool years are crucial in setting precedents and establishing patterns of behavior. You need to begin managing your child at a very young age.

Take heart, however, if your child is older, and you are worried that you have waited too long. Now is better than never. You have a difficult job ahead of you because you must help your child un-learn certain behaviors. However, you also have an older child who, in theory, can understand the reasoning behind the rules.

As you read this overview, many questions occurred to you, I know. Now I will explain certain aspects of the system in greater detail and provide you with scripts to use. I'll also address the most common "what-if" situations.

1. Identify privileges. What does your child like? Here are some suggestions:

- ☞ Painting a picture
- ☞ Watching a television show (each show is a separate privilege)
- ☞ Reading a book together
- ☞ Doing a puzzle
- ☞ Playing outside for a brief period of time (two blocks of ten minutes could be two separate privileges)
- ☞ Playing a card game or board game
- ☞ Enjoying a ten-minute block of time with you, uninterrupted
- ☞ Playing with a toy that is not always available
- ☞ Planning a snack or a meal (healthy choices can still be fun!)
- ☞ Being first or choosing first
- ☞ Playing in the tub
- ☞ Choosing clothes for a weekend day or special occasion

☞ Watching a video on the computer (e.g. dogs singing, funny babies, song from a movie)

☞ (Privileges should not be related to snack foods or buying things.)

Privileges are automatically given each day. Children do not have to earn the privileges. In the morning, say, "Which five privileges would you like today?" At the beginning, you may want to start with six, because they may be "counted out" (meaning "lost") quickly at the beginning. If a certain privilege will not work on a particular day, don't agree to it. Explain why you can't agree to it and suggest another time that it may work better.

If you don't have time to choose privileges in the morning, that's fine. You can start any-time, anywhere. If you want to start later in the day, instruct your child to choose a number of privileges appropriate for the amount of time left in the day. You or your child can write (or draw) one privilege on each sticky note. Display sticky notes where everyone can see them but where the children cannot reach them.

2. Maintain a businesslike tone of voice at all times when you are using the Privileges System. When you have to "count," use a business-

like, detached tone of voice. An angry voice or a threatening voice escalates tension.

3. Children can change their behavior very quickly. If you say "one" and the behavior doesn't stop immediately, wait about ten seconds before you say "two." *Do not talk at all between numbers.* Do not try to convince the child that it is in her best interest to change the behavior before you get to "three." She will realize that very quickly.

4. When you first begin to use the system, you must actually get to "three." She must lose some privileges in the early stages if she is to learn how the system works. Don't be afraid to get to "three."

5. When your counting reaches the number three, you say, "That's a three. The privilege you have lost is _____. You will get another chance tomorrow to have that privilege." Maintain the businesslike tone, even if you feel angry.

6. Once you get to three, you may see pouting, crying, or even yelling. Your response, in a

businesslike or sympathetic tone, is to say quietly, "I know you're sad. I'm sad too. I was looking forward to seeing you enjoy that privilege."

If the pouting, crying, or yelling does not stop quickly, you say, "I see you're choosing to use unacceptable behavior again. That's a one." Then begin the counting process again, if necessary. At first, losing multiple privileges in a short span of time is necessary. Even in the midst of a full-blown tantrum, you can still use this system. Just talk to the child as if she is listening, because she is.

If you are "counting out" one privilege after another and are starting to feel a loss of control, say, "I can see that you're not ready to make good choices right now. I'm going to leave the room. You can let me know when you're ready to make good choices again. Before I go, do you need a hug?"

Sometimes a child's level of frustration is so high that just the offer of a hug can help. Your calm demeanor and reassurance of love goes a long way in helping a child to become reasonable again.

Note: Some of the phrases I'm instructing you to use may not feel natural at first. Some of them use words that you don't use on a daily basis. Say them anyway. These words will show your child that a change has come and that you are dedicated to making change. Over time you will adapt the system (and its language) to fit your needs. At first, please say exactly what I have written. There are parents who type out their scripts in large, bold letters and tape them several places around the house. There is no shame in needing a reminder from time to time. And if your child is a reader, all the better. Don't hide the scripts. It's healthy for the child to see what you will say in a given situation.

7. If a child loses a privilege and leaves the room for some "quiet time," that's good! You have succeeded. Children need time to process what is happening. This system is intended to bring about change, and it will take time and practice.

If the child comes back to you and tries to negotiate a *return* of the privilege, utilize the "broken record" technique by saying, "I know you're feeling sad. I'm sad too. I was looking forward to you enjoying that privilege." Don't change the words. After saying that several times, you won't need to use the "broken record" technique anymore.

8. Baiting, pouting, whining, "sassiness," crying, begging, physical aggression, and disrespect are all reasons to count. Impatient behavior is not acceptable either. Before you begin counting, name the behavior. If you find a behavior unacceptable but can't name it easily, just label it "disrespectful."

Here come the scripts:

Adult: "You are being impatient, and you are baiting me right now. That's a one. If I reach the number three, you will lose a privilege." [Maintain businesslike tone.]

Child: "Which privilege?"

Adult: "I'll let you know if it becomes necessary." OR "The one you want the most."

Child: "Which one do you think I want the most?"

Adult: "I'm not discussing that right now. You need to focus on changing your behavior so that you don't lose *any* privileges."

(You have retained control of the situation and have not let your child engage you in an argument or a negotiation. It is perfectly acceptable to say, "I will not argue.")

9. Although this is a system where adults and children work together, it's natural for the child to try to gain the power. Watch for this. When you see it, you do not have to name it, because most children are not able to discuss power in a relationship. Just be aware that this is what is happening, and end it before it becomes a negotiation.

Example:

Child: "Which privilege will I lose first today?" or "Can I lose _____ first?"

Adult: "I'll let you know if it becomes necessary. Let's focus on having a great day and keeping our privileges. Which privilege would you like to enjoy next?"

10. Do not give the child an opportunity to "earn back" a privilege. That is confusing for the child, because it suggests that you will waver in your dedication to the system. If the child asks to earn back the privilege, you say, "I'm sad that you lost that privilege today too. Tomorrow is a new day. I know you'll make a better choice tomorrow." [Businesslike but sympathetic tone.]

11. What if you forget how far you counted or which privileges have been lost?

Guess who can provide you with that information? Your child! It's amazing how they are able to remember every detail. If you have more than one child, please don't allow one child to be a "tally" for another child. That will only lead to arguments among children.

Common situation: Your counting has reached "two" and the behavior ceases. Then, later in the day, the same behavior resurfaces. If it has been a while since you counted, then start again at "one." If you see this pattern recurring daily, count with less time between numbers so that you purposely get to "three" faster.

At the beginning, you may want to keep a note on the kitchen counter that reminds you when you counted, for what behavior, and which privilege was "counted out." Don't make this into a complicated system. If you need to keep a tally at first, that's just fine, but after a short time, it will become second nature to you and your child.

Sticky notes are the best way for everyone to keep track of which privileges remain. When a privilege has been enjoyed or "counted out," open an upper kitchen cabinet and put the post-it note inside.

12. Using the privileges: When you are planning privileges, think ahead to when they can be used. Don't agree to privileges that must all be used before bedtime. *Be sure to let the children use the privileges throughout the day.* You want them to be rewarded with privileges during the time that they may lose some too.

What if the privileges run out before the day is over? If the child has enjoyed the privileges already, or if they have been counted out, you may reach a situation where there are many hours left in the day and no privileges left. The best solution is to have the child choose more privileges. This will make her happy, and it will solve your problem.

Do not give back privileges that have been lost during that day. Ask the child to choose different ones. It's okay to say no to a privilege that the child suggests if there isn't enough time to enjoy it that day or if it is too messy or you just don't like it.

This is the time that you work together to come up with privileges that you both agree upon. Each child should choose a color for his sticky notes. Almost anything can be a privilege, even a block of time (ten minutes works well) where you give your undivided attention. No phone calls, no texting, no computer. If you have "left over" privileges at the end of the day, tell your child that she can use those privileges the following day, if she so chooses and you are agreeable. Don't agree to privileges that don't work for you!

13. When other adults are in charge: If your children will be staying with other adults, they can participate in the system too. Teach the other adult to name the offending behavior, count without yelling, and inform the child when "three" has been reached.

If the other adult "counts out" a privilege, the adult may supervise the loss of that privilege, or the adult may simply give you a report of how many privileges have been "counted out" and for what behaviors. Emphasize *no yelling* and *businesslike tone.* When you return, the other adult should give you the report while the child is present, if possible. This is not an opportunity for rebuttal from the child.

Example: After the other adult gives you a report, say to the child, "You have lost (number of) privileges, for doing____. I'll let you know shortly which privileges you've lost." Do not permit argument from your child. Say, "I left _____ in charge while I wasn't here. I trust his/her decisions. If he/she counted out ___ privileges, then that is the number of privileges you have lost."

14. Please do not attempt to use "time outs" while using the Privileges System. Trying to use the two systems together will be confusing to everyone involved.

Overall, remember...

Maintain a businesslike tone of voice. I cannot stress this enough. Even if you don't feel calm, pretend. The more quietly you speak, the harder they will listen.

Try to reduce the number of times you say "no" to your child. Children become immune to that. Instead, make a suggestion. You could also say, "I don't think that will work today" or "I'm disappointed to see..." or "I wish I could agree to that, but..."

This system is flexible. If you need to make a change, give the child some notice and then make the change. Some things are negotiable, some are not. If you make a change that is nonnegotiable, tell your children, "This is a decision that I make. You get to help choose your privileges, which is the most important part."

Use plenty of positive statements that point out and praise acceptable behavior. ("Thank you for your help." "Thank you for understanding." "You are really making progress.")

Creating the privileges together, calm counting, no yelling, enjoying privileges with your child, and plenty of praise create the recipe for a quiet and peaceful household. It will not necessarily be quiet at first, because your child will not willingly relinquish the power that he or she has held for a long time. But if you remain dedicated to change and want to stop yelling, then this is your plan. It's not expensive, it's not complicated, but it will change your life.

The Privileges System, Part II

Once you have used the Privileges System to eliminate the unacceptable behaviors, you may progress cautiously to Part II. It can be tempting to use Part II instead of Part I. Please trust me when I say that you must use Part I of the

Privileges System, where children lose privileges for unacceptable behavior, before you can progress to this higher level.

Part II involves "earning" privileges. We don't call them rewards or bribes. Whereas in Part I privileges were automatic and could be counted out, in Part II, you can say to your child, "Are you interested in earning a privilege?" This works best for children who are age five and older. When you ask if the child is interested in earning a privilege and he says "no," let it be. Don't coerce, don't use guilt, don't get angry. There will be a time when your child wants something. The next time he wants something say, "I think we can arrange that, if it's a privilege that you've earned." Ah-ha! You've got his attention now!

Part II is nothing more than a way to give your child privileges that he wants in return for behavior or action (or work!) that you want. Again, this is not intended to be a negotiation. You explain that the privilege is earned once the child completes the action. For example, "After you've made your bedroom look perfect, then you may play outside." Be careful with your words, however. Some children will attempt to circumvent your intention by using an alternate interpretation. If you say "make your bedroom look perfect" to one child, she may organize her closet and make her bed neatly. Another child may choose to interpret the phrase "make your room look perfect" as "toss everything under the bed and arrange the comforter to cover the mess."

Before privileges are awarded, check to be sure that they have indeed been earned. You don't need to say, "That was too fast. I don't believe that you really cleaned up your room." Instead say, "Okay, you're done? Great! Let's go take a look together." If the job has not been done satisfactorily, make observations, not criticisms. "I see some things still on the floor." OR "How about we straighten out the sheets a little better?" OR "I think if you look again, you might see some more work to be done." If you hear backtalk as a result, then count the unacceptable behavior. ("That's a 'one' for backtalk.") Part I and Part II of the Privileges System work beautifully together—if your child is ready. You could say, "To earn the privilege of playing outside, your room must look perfect. Come and get me when you're ready for us to look at it again."

Privileges Part II requires just as much determination as Part I, when you were counting more often. The two parts can be used together (as demonstrated above), but Part II is more than just bribing your child to do what you want him to do. You must think ahead and plan your terms. An older child may be able to suggest an earned privilege and the terms. If you feel that the suggestion is reasonable, go for it. If not, don't be bullied into accepting it. Older children appreciate the opportunity to offer suggestions.

Note: When children are earning privileges, be sure to stay away from phrases such as "If you do ___, I will give you ___." The reason that I say, "You may earn a privilege by..." is because I want to take the emphasis off of myself as the giver and taker of all things fun. Put the focus on the child's behavior and actions, not yours. Ultimately they will know that you are the one controlling the privileges, but it will cause much less friction between you and your child if you are not the focus. The privilege, and how to earn it, is the real focus.

Chapter Eleven:

The Balancing Act

When I grow up, I want to be...calm. It's what I aspire to be. I've dreamt of it for ages. My family would be so proud if I could achieve it.

A brand new mother said to me, "My baby has taken over my life. She *is* my life. Will I ever have a life again?" Don't you want to say, "Hallelujah! I'm not the only one who has this thought!" Let's face it: our children do tend to take over our lives. It's natural. They begin their journey in this world completely dependent on us. The thing is that some of us forget that as they grow, they are not completely dependent on us every second of every day anymore. They can make some choices for themselves, they can put their clothes on by themselves at some point, and they can even go to the bathroom without our help (though the condition of the bathroom afterward may not be as satisfactory as we might hope). In our goal of achieving calm, we must help our children achieve self-sufficiency. I know, I know. Easier said than done.

Recently our daughter started saying to us, at least once a day, "Nobody helps me anymore. I have to do everything. I clean up and nobody else does anything." She was serious. She really believed that she did everything around the house! I laughed at her (which wasn't very nice, I suppose), but it was just so ludicrous, considering that I was in the midst of planning her birthday party, sending out the invitations, buying the supplies, collecting birthday gifts for her, and overall just doing all of the glamorous jobs that go along with running a house.

In my spare time, I was buying clothes and shoes for her, since she had grown about four inches in the previous two weeks. Those things were in addition to helping her practice her reading, writing, and 'rithmetic. So when I asked her to put her toys away, she determined that nobody helped her anymore. The ironic thing is, with my child, when someone asks her if she needs help, the answer is always "no." I guess it's just nice to be asked.

Still, as painful as it is for everyone concerned, part of parenting is helping our children learn to function well without our help. Sometimes we don't want to, sometimes they don't want to, but if there is ever to be calm in our lives as parents, we have to show them how to wrap their towel around them when they get out of the bath/shower/pool, show them how to get a drink of water for themselves, and teach them which clothes match other clothes so they don't leave the house looking like miniature clowns. Self-sufficiency ultimately leads to calm, but the path isn't an easy one.

The balancing act of parenting is one that never goes away. It begins with a newborn, trying to get the bottles made before the baby wakes up and needs to be changed, and it continues for the rest of our lives. One of my mentors said to me, "The hardest thing about being a parent is that once you feel you've mastered it and maybe feel that it isn't so difficult after all, they change!" As they grow, they constantly develop new "issues," and we have to constantly figure out how to help them figure out those new issues. And we as parents have to balance their needs against our sanity.

Working Toward "Calm"

Because our kids are part of us, we are so connected to them that it feels wrong sometimes to send them out into their lives to fend for themselves. We don't know when is the right time to let go a little. My suggestion is: Give it a try. See how it goes. Parenting is all about trial and error, and though we don't like to admit it, we do err sometimes. However, we don't know what our children can do until we give them a chance to try! I wondered when was the right age for my daughter to wash her own hair and to graduate to taking showers rather than baths and to swim without floaties. And for that matter, when is the proper time to teach a child how to ride a bicycle? When should they be allowed to pour milk on their cereal by themselves? How old is old enough to attend a sleepover? You could add to this list of parenting mysteries, I'm sure.

The parenting books don't answer these questions. If you read parenting books with the hope of having any of these types of questions answered, you will come away with a vague answer that suggests to you that you should allow your child to proceed when it feels right to you.

When it feels right to me? When is that? There are times when nothing feels right to me!

Going back to the common sense approach, though, I remind myself that we have to approach things slowly, without judgment, and talk about what's going to happen before it happens. This falls under the heading of treating children with respect too. When I decided that I was really tired of the bath ritual and wanted my daughter to begin taking showers, we talked about it. I supervised her about ten times. She didn't like the supervision (she never does), but it was necessary. I remember that once she mastered the showering part, she didn't want to turn the water off by herself because she was afraid that the water would change temperatures when she did. I showed her that the shower temperature "adjuster" was located in a different place than the "shower turner-offer." We practiced together, with her hand on top of mine. She did it! She does it!

As with everything else involving a child, I must be nearby to be sure that things go smoothly (particularly where water is concerned), and I need to consider her maturity level before we undertake a new adventure in self-sufficiency, but once the process is accomplished, we both feel better. She feels like she's becoming more independent, and I feel...*calm.*

When you suspect that it may be time for your child to reach for some self-sufficiency or attempt a new task, ask yourself these questions:

- How long have we been doing this task together? Is my child familiar with the steps?
- Is my child physically tall enough or strong enough to operate the "tools" necessary to complete the job?
- What would the consequences be if his first attempt did not go well?
- How can I break this task into steps so that we share the responsibility at first?
- When is the best time to explain to him that he is going to begin doing this task by himself? (I would strongly suggest a time that is not just before the task is to begin or when the child is tired or hungry.)
- Is there a way that I can present this idea to my child as a "privilege" he has earned?

* We always want to put a positive spin on self-sufficiency.

So on your journey to calm, one of the first steps can be to help your child achieve self-sufficiency in some areas. One area at a time. With plenty of praise and reassurance. The beauty of this approach is that it really doesn't change much over time. We always need to work on becoming self-sufficient, no matter how old we become, and the process is the same regardless of age.

Adjust Your Expectations

I'm really good at telling other people to adjust their expectations. I hear myself say it to other people, and it sounds great. Maybe it's just me, but I don't think I know very many people with low expectations. Do you? I have noticed that the few people I've encountered who have reasonable expectations are much more calm than me. Unusually low expectations can sometimes indicate depression, but for the purposes of this book, let's focus on those who have reasonable expectations and are joyful. I have an aunt who falls into this category—reasonable expectations, calm, and joyful.

I'm sure that she is not always calm and joyful, but I've known her for a long time, and she has been my idol for many years. Maybe she would tell you differently, but what I have observed is this: she does not play the "what-if" game and therefore does not practice the art of anticipating every negative consequence of every action. She is not afraid of life—she just lives it; she treasures children and their antics; she takes joy in occasions and makes an occasion of times that otherwise might not be. (She also brings people iced sugar cookies, which is an endearing quality of its own!)

People who do not have such high expectations are people to be admired. They are the ones who teach us to simply enjoy what we have been given. Reasonable expectations are so important in parenting. We live in a world that moves too fast and expects too much. It's no wonder that we, as parents, have difficulty balancing all of it sometimes. When life overwhelms us, our children become sources of frustration. "Can I have fry-fries?" "Can I bring sixteen books in the car?" "Can Daddy ride me on his back?" These are questions that might have been cute if they were asked at a time when we were not rushed or stressed. But when life overwhelms us and we've overbooked ourselves and our children, questions like these do not tend to illicit "cute" answers.

As a society, we have super-high expectations, which carry over into our parenting. To counteract this problem, I propose that we simplify our lives as much as possible, adjust our expectations, and revel in the beauty of life. (Are you hearing a soundtrack in the background? A little hippie music from the '70s perhaps?) Seriously, we cannot be good parents if we subject our children to expectations that are too high. Don't overbook yourself and your kids! Don't succumb to parental peer pressure (e.g. enrolling your kids in everything imaginable)! Don't let our high-tech, fast-moving culture dictate the type of parent you become. Parenting is, by nature, a slow-moving process. It requires you to know your child and think about his or her abilities. It requires all of us to expect of our children what they can actually achieve.

To help us achieve balance in our lives as parents, we need to make time for the important things, which begins with setting reasonable goals and expectations for ourselves and for our children. We also need to make occasions out of things that would otherwise not be, and to those occasions...we need to bring iced sugar cookies.

Managing the Questions

"Mommy, do bugs wear boots?" This is what my daughter asked me one day as we were driving home in the rain. I said, "What would make you ask such a question?" She replied, "Well, bugs are so small, and if it rains hard, and they have to cross over a puddle, their feet will always get wet!"

There are some questions that we treasure. All parents hear questions that are just plain funny. When you hear those questions, write them down. Those questions are some of the joys of parenthood. They make you smile, and because of that, they are a gift. Write them down.

Still, writing down the cute questions is not sufficient advice for a parent who is about to head for the hills because she is being questioned beyond imagination. Imagination does have something to do with it, from the child's point of view. They are constantly imagining, "What if..." Imagining consequences make up a good part of their day, so it makes sense that they are constantly asking us, "I know this would never happen, but what if it did?" Today my husband was asked what would happen if the automatic pool cleaner jumped out of the pool and got away. He looked at me as if to say, "The questions! How do I make them stop?!" To anyone wondering the same thing, here is my suggestion: don't answer all of the questions.

Sometimes I tell my daughter that she can ask me five more questions until dinner time. I give her five index cards, numbered one to five, and each time she asks a question, I take a card back. Kids don't mind this as much as you think they would. First of all, kids tend to tolerate anything that seems like a game. Second, they get to manage the questions they ask, so they maintain at least some control. Once my daughter has asked her five questions and she asks another, I simply say, "Oops. That was a question." Usually after a few seconds of pouting, she goes off to find something else to do. Or someone else to ask. Hey, when it comes to questions, it's every adult for himself.

Another thing to remember is that when your child asks constant questions, it is her way of initiating conversation. It used to make me nuts when my child would ask questions about topics that we had covered before. Then I realized: she wants to talk to me and doesn't know how to start a conversation. So I say to her, "What should we talk about now?" Yes, that's *me* asking a question, but sometimes it keeps us from covering the same material we covered an hour ago!

Yet another approach is to divert your child's attention away from the questions by saying, "Let's play a game." Where you go from there is your decision. If you're at home, you could play an actual card game or board game. If you're in the car (which is where I find that the questioning often runs rampant), I invent a game. Sometimes I say, "Let's make up a story. I'll start by saying a sentence, and then you continue the story." Depending on the age of your child, you may have to be the player who moves the plot of the story along, but when the story ends, your child will feel a sense of accomplishment.

You can also do "story problems" involving math computation. Children are sometimes intimidated by story problems (word problems) when they are in school, but in a more casual atmosphere, they can be fun. Here's an example: "Do you see how there are four cars ahead of us in line at the stoplight? When the light turns green and two of the cars turn right, how many cars will be in front of us?" Certainly you must adjust your story problems to fit your child's ability, but this is a way to practice math without them realizing that they are doing so.

If you are at home, use more tangible props. Say, "Please go get five pair of your shoes and bring them to the kitchen and line them up in a row." Once that is done, ask, "How many shoes do you have? What if your friend who wears the same size shoes as you do came into the kitchen and put on a pair of your shoes? Then how many shoes would you have?" You can ask your child to pick up the shoes and move them to another room to demonstrate subtraction.

There is no end to the number of ways you can distract a child from asking questions *ad nauseam.* Children can be distracted—no doubt about that. Beware, however: distraction is not a cure for questioning. The questions will be back. They're never far away. When they do come back, do your best to embrace them as evidence that you have a child with intellectual curiosity. That's a cause for celebration, right? Right!

Maintaining the "You"

Your child is your whole world, but he cannot be your whole life. Yes, you read that correctly. When you are telling someone that your child is your "whole world," you are really saying, "I love this child so much that I can't even explain it. This child has filled my heart and my soul, and I can't imagine my life without him in it." By saying that your child is your "whole world," you are summarizing your feelings. I've done it.

There is a difference, though, when the child who is your "whole world" becomes your "whole life." This happened to me, I admit it. When our daughter came to us, we had been through a rough time. My mother had been gravely ill for two years, and the process that we went through to get a child was heart-wrenching. The joy that I felt during the first few months that I was a mom was like no other joy I have ever felt. Not only was I so busy learning to take care of an infant (it took me two hours to get out the door the first time I took her out!), but it was my honor and privilege to do all the mundane tasks that mothers do. That was it. She was my world, and my world was happy. Not to mention that after having gone through a difficult two years with no humorous stories to tell, it was delightful to finally be able to tell stories about what my child was doing, seeing, "accomplishing." People didn't ask me how *I* was doing; they asked me how *she* was doing. And I never minded it for a moment.

Time passed, and our family needed even more of the healing balm that a small child provides. Six months after our daughter came to us, my mother-in-law became gravely ill too. Never before had our family needed something happy to talk about. To focus on. The pain our family was enduring by having both grandmothers so sick is nearly indescribable, even now. Our daughter was the only sunshine in our lives for a very long time.

With all that was happening in our family it was only natural that our daughter became my "whole world." But after my mother-in-law passed away in 2008 and my mother passed away in 2010, I was left feeling lost. I remember thinking, "Who am I?" The better question would have been, "Who do I want to be?" I had been a teacher and a lawyer, I was a daughter, a wife, a sister, a friend, but I came to realize that my daughter had not only become my "whole world," she had become my "whole life." Certainly it was not her fault. It just happened. But I realized that I had to be my own person, just as I was slowly teaching her to become her own person. How better to teach her than show her what it means to be your own person?

The book you are reading right now is the outcome of some of my soul searching. I have always loved to write and have always wanted to publish a book. I also dream, as I write this, of the day that my daughter can say that her mom is an "author." There are so many more things that I want to be, like a speaker of foreign languages, a traveler, a classroom teacher (again), and probably many more things that I haven't even thought of yet.

One of the things I've learned about parenting is that to be a good parent, we have to be other things too. Things that satisfy *us*, not just our children. We cannot depend on them to fill our lives for us. Not only will it likely make us crabby in the short term, it will leave us lonely and unfulfilled when our children become the self-sufficient human beings that we are raising them to be.

Remember the old phrase "Get a life!" Well, go ahead, do it. By enhancing your sense of yourself, your children will actually benefit. If you pursue interests for you and only you, the "break" that you get from your children will make you more patient and more appreciative of the little ones who can comfortably remain your "whole world."

Chapter Twelve:
Practicing Parenting

Parenting is like walking in flip-flops. It takes practice. Think back to when you learned to walk in flip-flops. You fell off a few times, didn't you? Be honest now. Not only that, your flip-flop probably came apart and you went flying into someone eating an ice cream cone on the board-walk, didn't you? Okay, maybe that was just me.

Still, the analogy holds. Parenting takes practice. Another way to phrase it is that it's all trial and error. There are no two children alike, who reach the same milestones at the exact same time, and who respond to the same reasoning in the exact same way. Therefore, it's all trial and error.

A new mother recently told me that there are nights when she crawls into bed and breathes a sigh before falling asleep, and her last thought is, *I don't know if I can do all of this again tomorrow.* Though I'm not sure she was joking, I had to chuckle because I doubt if there is a parent anywhere who doesn't have the same thought from time to time. The reality that should comfort us is that we won't have to do the exact same thing again tomorrow. It will change. It always does. Our experiences today have taught us some of what we will need to know tomorrow.

Doctors practice medicine, lawyers practice law, and parents practice parenting. It's funny how the first two are commonly heard in conversation, while the third one is not. No one says that they are "practicing parenting" because, for some unknown reason, our culture leads parents to believe that they don't need practice—that they are immediate experts once they become parents. I'm here to tell you that parenting takes practice.

It takes practice to let some things go. It takes practice to pick your battles, it takes practice to watch other parents do their thing and decide whether their approach will work for you. We teach our kids that everything takes practice, and we need to remind ourselves of the same thing. We are aiming for progress here. My mother used to say, "Kids don't come with a book of instructions." So true. It means that you do the best you can every day, and that's all anyone can expect. More importantly, it's all that you can expect of yourself.

Often, when the day comes to an end, I wish that I had been more patient. I have said to many people, "God is trying to teach me patience, and I haven't learned it yet." But I'm working on it. Our children have to practice every new skill that they learn; what makes us think that we shouldn't have to practice, too?

So, once we've practiced, how do we know how we're doing? We don't get report cards. Truthfully, how many of us would really want to see that report card? Usually we know what we're doing well and what needs improvement. Ironically, it's our children who give us feedback on our parenting.

I'm not talking about the times they shout, "I hate you! You're mean!" That's not a genuine report card. That's anger. The genuine report card comes at a time when your child is calm, when you're having a good chat, and your child gives you a bit of feedback. My friend's daughter said to her one day, "Mom, thanks for giving me a brain." Bingo. A report card. She wasn't being literal—she wasn't really thanking her mom for her brain. She was thanking my friend for teaching her how to make decisions for herself and take pride in her decisions. She was thanking her mom for helping her to become a mature young lady who didn't get caught up in the silliness of other girls in her class.

My daughter, at age four, said to me, "Mom, I forget sometimes that you love me, but today I remembered." She remembered because she lost a privilege! She remembered because I tell her often that my job is to help her become a kind young lady, and on that particular day she had not been a kind young lady. What she remembered was that I don't make rules to be mean; I make rules to help her become a kind young lady. I was proud of her when she told me that, and let's face it, I was walking pretty proud that day too. Sometimes it's okay for us to think to ourselves, "I did good." That particular day, I guess I had done good.

Stand Back and Soak It In

Many years ago when I was planning my wedding, I remember going to a bridal shop to look at wedding gowns. I stopped by quickly, without intending to try on any gowns, but not surprisingly, I found myself in the fitting room with at least six gowns. As it turned out, one of those gowns was *the one*, but I digress...

As most brides-to-be, I could hardly believe that I was looking at myself in a wedding dress. I looked like a princess. I had dreamed of this for so long; I was engaged to marry a prince. (He still is, by the way.) Anyway, as I was standing in the main area of the shop, the area containing the huge mirrors, I noticed an elderly lady sitting on a velvet couch in the background. She smiled at me; I returned the smile. Then she motioned for me to come over. Being a person who always believes in respecting one's elders, I gladly approached her. Here is what she said to me: "On your special day, when your friends and loved ones are dancing and celebrating, take a moment to stand back and just soak it all in. Don't let the time get away from you without truly seeing what is happening. Look at what you've created and what is happening around you."

I assured her that I would do as she suggested, and I did. I could see that she was a wise lady of considerable experience, and I knew that I was not. A year later, when our special day came, I did what the stranger in the bridal shop told me to do. I stood back and soaked it in. I reveled in the beauty, thanked the heavens for the blessings in my life, and vowed to always remember the beauty of that time. Not only that, in the nineteen years since then, I have passed on the same wisdom to many, many brides-to-be.

So why write about a "bridal" story in a parenting book? Because that lady, who took the time to talk to me, taught me a lesson that is equally as pertinent for parents as it is for newlyweds. "Stand back and soak it in." It is easier to do this on a wedding day, because it is just one day. As a parent, we cannot stand back and "soak in" every moment of every day, or we wouldn't get anything done! Our children seem to change so fast when we study photos that have been taken over time, but on a daily basis, things seem pretty much the same. The chores, the challenges. They don't seem to change all that fast. Sometimes we just don't want to "soak it all in" because it seems a little tedious to be "soaked in" every day.

Still, heed the advice of the dowager in the bridal shop, and be sure to pay attention to the wonder that surrounds you. Set aside the tedium, push that to the back of your mind, and soak in something about your day as a parent that will stay with you for years to come. Is it an "impish" look? Is it a new word that your child learned? Is it a note that the teacher sent home telling you how much she enjoyed your child today? Whatever it is, soak it all in.

This is a parenting skill that takes practice, just like all of the other skills. If you practice celebrating the gifts you have been given, it will be much easier to do it all again tomorrow. The lady in the bridal shop taught me a lot that day in 1991. Her advice was not just advice for a bride-to-be. It was advice for parents too. I never learned the lady's name that day, nor did I ever see her again. Still, I will never forget her, and wherever she is, I humbly thank her for her wisdom.

The List

I love lists. They're orderly. They're concise, and they are full of great wisdom that you can quote. I especially love a book that ends with a list. I hope you do too. These are the things that you should do when you are too tired to remember the things that you should do.

1. "Whatever works." Remember that parenting is all about trial and error, and every child, along with every situation, requires creativity. If your approach is safe and effective, don't concern yourself with whether you're doing what the books say or what everyone else does. Be reasonable, and use a lot of common sense and as much humor as you can manage.

2. "Know your child." Observe your child and create your own objective ideas about what he or she needs. Labels that others assign to your child can be hurtful or helpful depending on how they're used.

3. "Above all, play." We need to make time to play, to be silly, to have fun. You will find that you connect with your child better when you show him or her that you can let go of your serious side from time to time and just simply play. Children are funny. Embrace this. Treasure it. It's nature's way of preserving your sanity.

4. "Honesty is the best policy, unless it isn't." It is absolutely crucial that you teach your child to tell the truth, but as an adult, you know that there are a few times when stretching the truth is the best thing for everyone concerned.

5. "Learn by all means possible." Whether you are well-educated by traditional standards is not all that relevant when it comes to parenting. As a parent, learn from books, other parents, teachers, strangers, experience, and failure. If one approach works, repeat it. If it doesn't, tweak it.

6. "Celebrate your successes, and pass them on..." Don't be afraid to admit that you could

use some help, and don't be shy about offering your help to another parent. If you offer to help, you may be turned down, but offer anyway. We parents need to stick together.

7. "Adjust your expectations." Love unconditionally and acknowledge that you cannot control your child's behavior. You can try your best to "shape" behavior, but control it? No way.

8. "Expect the unexpected, and buy plenty of wire cutters." Life is all about surprises. We like some of them more than others, but as parents, we will get a healthy dose of the unexpected. Why buy wire cutters? Because every toy is wired into its box so thoroughly these days that you need wire cutters more than you ever have before. Don't just expect the unexpected; expect to *need* wire cutters!

9. "Always RSVP." When you RSVP to an invitation, you are being courteous and clear about your intentions. Everyone appreciates clarity. It shows your children how to treat others with respect, and let's be honest: it just makes you look good.

10. "Tomorrow is another day." If today was a bad day, congratulations! You get another chance tomorrow. If today was a good day,

congratulations! You get another chance. Stay optimistic and always keep learning.

11. "We are all teachers, adults and children alike." We learn from them; they learn from us. For either or both to happen, we must pay attention. Be present for your life, and be present for your children.

12. "You *will* make a difference." You can bring each day to a close knowing that you will always make a difference in the life of another human being. You are important. You matter. You're a parent.

Made in the USA
Charleston, SC
23 April 2012